DAVID GLUSS

D0712947

**APPLICATIONS OF**
**OPTIMAL CONTROL THEORY**
**TO COMPUTER CONTROLLER DESIGN**

# APPLICATIONS OF
# OPTIMAL CONTROL THEORY
# TO COMPUTER CONTROLLER DESIGN

William S. Widnall

RESEARCH MONOGRAPH No. 48
THE M.I.T. PRESS,
CAMBRIDGE, MASSACHUSETTS, AND LONDON, ENGLAND

This work was prepared under DSR Project 55-23850,
sponsored by the Manned Spacecraft Center of the National
Aeronautics and Space Administration through Contract NAS 9-4065.

The publication of this work does not constitute approval by the
National Aeronautics and Space Administration of the findings or
conclusions contained herein. It is published only for the exchange
and stimulation of ideas.

Copyright    ©    1968 by
The Massachusetts Institute of Technology

Printed by Halliday Lithograph Corporation,
West Hanover, Massachusetts, and
bound in the United States of America by
The Riverside Press, Cambridge, Massachusetts

All rights reserved. No part of this book may be
reproduced or utilized in any form or by any means,
electronic or mechanical, including photocopying,
recording, or by any information storage and retrieval
system, without permission in writing from the publisher.

Library of Congress catalog card number: 68-14445

# FOREWORD

This is the forty-eighth volume in the M. I. T. Research
Monograph Series published by the M. I. T. Press. The
objective of this series is to contribute to the professional
literature a number of significant pieces of research, larger
in scope than journal articles but normally less ambitious than
finished books. We believe that such studies deserve a wider
circulation than can be accomplished by informal channels, and
we hope that this form of publication will make them readily
accessible to research organizations, libraries, and independent
workers.

Howard W. Johnson

# PREFACE

Over the past two decades, since control system design was first approached as an optimization problem, a steady flow of intensive research has produced analytical and numerical design procedures which give great insight into the nature of efficient control systems. There continues to be, however, a large gap between the theoretical progress of optimal control theory in the literature and the design tools used by control system engineers in practice. The intent of this book is to further develop and exploit linear quadratic cost optimal control theory and the use of modern digital computers to design practical feedback control systems. Special emphasis is given to the problem of computer control of continuous systems, where the allowable complexity of a control computer program is limited by execution speed or available memory. Realistic examples derived mostly from spacecraft control problems are used to illustrate the suggested techniques and to demonstrate the success of the approaches. It is hoped that this book will be of great value to engineers responsible for the design of computer controllers who wish to use the latest analytical and numerical design techniques.

This book is a publication of the author's doctoral thesis "On the design of nearly optimal linear time-varying sampled-data stochastic controllers," submitted to the M.I.T. Department of Aeronautics and Astronautics in September 1966. The author is indebted to Professors Wallace E. Vander Velde of M.I.T., Arthur E. Bryson of Harvard and M.I.T., and James E. Potter of M.I.T. for their many comments and suggestions while providing direction to this research. In addition, the M.I.T. Instrumentation Laboratory, directed by Dr. C. Stark Draper, has provided a stimulating environment for this research. To mention only a few in the Apollo Mission Development Division of Dr. Richard H. Battin, the author wishes to thank Edward M. Copps, Dr. Frederick H. Martin, and Gilbert Stubbs for numerous discussions concerning onboard computer control of the Apollo spacecraft. Current design problems at the laboratory motivated the choice of many of the examples given in this work. Dr. Donald C. Fraser provided valuable computer programs for the frequency domain analysis of constant-coefficient sampled-data systems. The computation facilities of the laboratory were freely available for developing the numerical illustrations. The manuscript was typed by Nancy Stone Jordan and Jolyn Ward McNeil. The figures were prepared by Robert E. Weatherbee. The Apollo Mission Development staff and the laboratory computer facilities are supported by the Manned Spacecraft Center of the National Aeronautics and Space Administration.

The author wishes to thank his wife, Dr. Sheila Evans Widnall, for encouraging this effort and for listening to many of the technical ideas as they developed. Thanks also go to the Apollo Digital Simulation Group at the Instrumentation Laboratory under Dr. James S. Miller for relieving the author of his staff responsibilities so that he could undertake this effort.

November 1967                              William S. Widnall

# CONTENTS

**APPLICATIONS OF**
**OPTIMAL CONTROL THEORY**
**TO COMPUTER CONTROLLER DESIGN**

# Chapter 1

## Introduction

In the field of control system design, recent research has produced analytical design procedures which give great insight into the nature of efficient control systems. Much of this work started with Wiener (1949), who suggested that the search for an efficient system should be formulated as an optimization problem. Wiener used a mean-squared error criterion to evaluate how well the output of a system approached the desired output. Assuming that the input to the system and the desired output were stationary random processes, Wiener discovered an explicit design procedure for finding the optimal linear system – optimum in the sense that the quadratic error criterion is minimized. The optimal linear system has an impulse response function which satisfies an integral equation over a semi-infinite interval. (This type of equation is now called a Wiener-Hopf equation). Wiener provided the solution to this integral equation by a method of manipulating its Fourier transform, called spectral factorization.

Before Wiener, control system design was largely an art, rather than an engineering science. Simple feedback compensation would be proposed and adjusted until a reasonably satisfactory design was discovered. This procedure works well in simple applications, but in large complex systems the trial-and-error approach is not satisfactory. Too many permutations and combinations of compensation are possible, so an effective efficient design may never be discovered. Following Wiener's lead, the field of optimal control theory has attempted to evolve a radically different approach to the design problem. The design engineer is to devote considerable attention to formulating the design problem accurately. He must develop mathematical models for the plant to be controlled as well as the disturbances driving the plant. He must know the nature of the measurements of the plant state that will be available, including any sources of noise which will corrupt the measurements. All the various competing control objectives must be gathered together into an analytical statement of the cost of operating the plant. It is the goal of optimal control theory to assist the design engineer at this point by producing explicitly the control system design which will minimize the cost.

A general design procedure for nonlinear plants and arbitrary cost functions perhaps cannot be found. But for some less ambitious problem statements, excellent optimal design procedures have been found. The most successful branch of optimal control theory, in common with Wiener, considers linear plants whose operating cost can be expressed by a quadratic function. (A review of many other branches of optimal control theory is given by Bryson (1966)).

A general result of linear quadratic cost control theory is that the order of the theoretically optimal controller is equal to the order of the process being controlled. Unfortunately a practical optimal design must minimize more than only operating errors. The economic cost of a design must be considered. Reliability must be considered. The time required to build the controller must be considered. Generally the simpler the design, the easier it will be to meet specifications on cost, schedule, and reliability. Thus a practical design often must have a low-order controller matched to the high-order plant. Phillips (see James, Nichols, and Phillips (1947)) proposed a systematic procedure for the practical design problem: The design engineer still must carefully develop a mathematical model for the process and for the cost of operating the process. But now he must propose a simplified controller design. He can leave several gains or other parameters in the design unspecified. Phillips showed how the mean quadratic cost can be expressed as an explicit nonlinear function of the unspecified gains. The optimization of the simplified design therefore reduces to a search for the parameter values which will minimize the mean cost function.

Franklin (1955) extended Wiener's synthesis method to sampled-data systems. In place of the Fourier transform for continuous systems, Franklin used the z-transform to represent sampled-data systems. Again the method of spectral factorization was used to solve for the optimal linear system. A similar design theory was later developed independently by Chang (1958).

Much of the work up to this point was summarized in the book by Newton, Gould, and Kaiser (1957). NGK reviewed the Wiener stationary least-squares continuous linear system and extended the theory to include several constraints imposed by practical systems. Conceptually the cascade compensation of Wiener would include the inverse of the plant dynamics followed by a filter having the transfer function desired for the overall system. If, however, the transfer function of the plant was not minimum phase, then the inverse filter could not be realized as a stable system. NGK were able to solve for the optimal compensation in this case of a nonminimum-phase plant. Another difficulty encountered was the saturation of control variables. Where the plant has lag (integration), the inverse compensation must have lead (differentiation). Thus the controller which minimizes the output error of the plant will probably call for arbitrarily large control signals to achieve the objective. NGK demonstrated a solution to this difficulty: To constrain the RMS value of the control signal, the square of the control signal is added to the square of the output error, by means of an undetermined Lagrange multiplier. The optimal linear system can be found which minimizes the mean value of this more general performance index. This optimal design will be a function of the Lagrange multiplier. For the optimal design, one can compute the mean-square value of the control signal as an analytic nonlinear function of the Lagrange multiplier. One then solves this function for the value of the multiplier which will yield the optimal design exactly meeting the control activity specification.

The design procedure of Phillips was applied by Robinson (1957) to sampled-data systems: The optimal choices for the coefficients in the z-transform of a trial compensation are those which minimize an explicit formula for the mean quadratic cost. A new motivation for simplified design exists in the case of sampled-data systems. Today, the design of a sampled-data controller is often synonymous with the programming of a given computer to control the process. In searching for the best control computer program one must consider the constraints imposed by the limitations of the computer. One limitation discussed by Robinson is the arithmetic speed of the computer. Since a finite amount of time is required to process the instructions in a program, it follows that a complicated program will require more time to execute than a simple program. Thus it is quite possible that a simplified control computer program, by permitting a shorter sample interval to be used, can exercise tighter control on the process than a more complicated program.

3

Up to this point the literature of linear least-squares controllers was restricted to constant-coefficient systems. One could design explicitly the constant-coefficient system for a stochastic environment which would have minimum mean-squared error in the steady state, or one could design explicitly the constant-coefficient system for the deterministic noise-free problem which would have minimum integral squared error. But the best gains for steady-state performance are not necessarily the best gains for transient response. Attempts at extending the frequency domain techniques to handle nonstationary processes and time-varying controllers were only partially successful. New techniques were then developed in the time-domain which led to a rapid expansion of linear quadratic cost optimal control theory. The philosophical basis for the time domain techniques was popularized by Bellman (1957). The method, which he named "dynamic programming," utilized a sequential principle of optimality: The best choice of control action to complete the operating period does not depend on the control action which was used prior to the present instant. With this principle, one can in theory construct the optimal control policy as a memoryless function of the present state of the process. Unfortunately the "curse of dimensionality" makes impractical the synthesis of a controller for an arbitrary nonlinear process. One in theory must store, for each stage in time, a table of the optimal control value for every possible value of process state. If there are more than two or three state variables in the process, then for even the most crude quantization of state levels, the number of entries required in the table becomes enormous.

But in the case of a linear plant with a quadratic error criterion the "curse of dimensionality" was overcome. Kalman and Koepcke (1958) applied the technique of dynamic programming to the deterministic noise-free sampled-data controller problem. For a linear plant and with an integral squared error performance criterion they showed that the optimal control value, to be held until the next sample instant, is a linear time-varying memoryless function of the state of the process at the present sample instant. The optimal time variations of the controller gains are a function of the time-to-go to the terminal instant. For the operating period sufficiently before the terminal time, the optimal gains may become constant. Thus Kalman and Koepcke's solution provided, as a special case, an alternate synthesis procedure for the constant-coefficient optimal transient response

4

design problem. If only pencil and paper are available, the spectral factorization method of solution is the less tedious method. But if a digital computer is available, the iterative time-domain algorithm is easier to program, and the computer will do the tedious work.

To implement the Kalman-Koepcke controller, one must construct in some way all the state variables of the plant. It was not obvious how one might do this in a real-time controller with only noisy measurements of some of the state components in the plant. Kalman (1960) derived a linear time-varying estimator for the state variables, which has the property that the error in the estimate of each component of the state has minimum mean-squared value. The structure of the Kalman estimator is conceptually very simple. The estimator includes a simulation of the state transitions of the actual process. That is, the best estimate of the plant state is extrapolated forward in time according to the known dynamics of the process. At a measurement time, the best prediction of what the measurement should be is compared with the actual noisy measurement. The measurement discrepancy is weighted according to the relative strength of the current estimate uncertainty as compared to the known variance of the measurement noise. The weighted measurement error is used to apply corrections to the estimates of each component of the state. The Kalman estimator is often time-varying because as initial estimates of the state variables are improved, the optimal weights for the measurements decrease. In some problems, for an operating period sufficiently far from the initial time, the Kalman estimator may become a constant-coefficient system. The recursive formulas, for finding the optimal estimator as a function of the time-elapsed since estimation was initiated, provide as a special case an alternate solution to Wiener's stationary filter problem. And again Kalman's solution is easier to program for computation. Kalman and Bucy (1961) soon extended the recursive estimator to continuous systems.

It seemed reasonable that an efficient controller might be synthesized by cascading a Kalman estimator with a Kalman-Koepcke controller. The estimator would provide good estimates of each component of the plant state from the noisy feedback measurements; the controller would operate on these estimates, as though they were perfect, and would provide the control signal. Joseph and Tou (1961) were able to prove that this cascade synthesis actually is optimal, in that the mean value of the cost integral is minimized by this design. Additional discussion of the sampled-data controller separated-synthesis theorem is given by Gunckel and Franklin (1963). Potter (1964) proved an analogous theorem for continuous stochastic controllers.

Johansen (1964) considered the design of simplified time-varying continuous stochastic controllers. Extending the design philosophy of Phillips to time-varying systems, Johansen developed a numerical procedure for finding the time-variation of several unspecified coefficients, in an assumed controller structure, which would minimize the mean cost.

In this dissertation we explore the utility of optimal linear time-varying stochastic quadratic-cost sampled-data control theory, as an aid to the designer of a computer-limited control computer program. In Chapter 2 we provide a systematic procedure for evaluating the performance of any linear control computer program, whether optimal or not optimal. In Chapter 3 we review the details of optimal controller synthesis. We note that the Joseph and Tou synthesis yields an optimal controller which is not unique. We will show that one can transform the optimal control computer program into a (unique) canonical form which will minimize the required controller computations. In Chapter 4 we demonstrate several indirect applications of optimal controller synthesis to the design of computer-limited controllers. We can compute bounds on the possible performance of computer-limited designs. We can design simplified time-varying controllers by synthesizing optimal solutions to simpler problems. We can with ease design efficient constant-coefficient stochastic controllers using the algorithms for optimal time-varying controller synthesis. In Chapter 5 we consider the optimization of simplified time-varying sampled-data controllers. We use the design philosophy of Phillips in a way similar to that of Johansen. But we limit the unspecified nature of the time-varying coefficients to a finite number of parameters, and we work with the unique canonical form controllers. These modifications in Johansen's approach permit better convergence to an optimized design. We use the descent method of Davidon (1959) to search for the values of the free parameters which yield the minimum mean cost. In these different chapters we have included some realistic numerical examples of the basic ideas to demonstrate the utility of the theory. As a by-product we have developed a package of computer programs, which are of a general nature, for assisting in the design of control computer programs.

Chapter 2

## The Evaluation of Linear Sampled-Data Controllers

## 2.1 Introduction

The designer of a controller for a complicated system must take into account many factors: the dynamic equations of the plant, the measurements of the plant state available for control information, the objectives of the control action, likely initial conditions, desired terminal conditions, disturbances forcing the plant state, noises in the measurements. Any trial controller design must be evaluated in this stochastic environment to verify whether or not it performs in a satisfactory manner.

In this chapter we discuss a computational procedure for predicting the average closed-loop performance of a linear plant and a linear sampled-data controller. In Section 2.2 we review the mathematical description of the continuous stochastic process. This includes the state space representation of the linear plant and the quadratic cost integral. In Section 2.3 we show that the continuous stochastic process may be characterized by a sampled-data state-transition representation. The integral cost formula may be replaced by a discrete summation formula. In Section 2.4 we develop the calculations required to evaluate the mean cost, as well as the covariance of the combined plant and controller state space at the sampling instants. In Section 2.5 we show how to compute the time histories of the mean-squared values of the quantities of interest between the sampling instants. These procedures can be programmed into a general-purpose design package (Appendix C). Such a package of digital computer programs can be of great usefulness to the design engineer. As an illustration of these computational procedures, in Section 2.6 we evaluate the short burn performance of a spacecraft closed-loop steering-control law which is used in the Apollo project.

7

## 2.2 Mathematical Description of the Continuous Stochastic Process

In evaluating a control process we are interested in certain components of the state vector. For example, in an attitude control problem, we would be interested in the deviation of the vehicle attitude away from a desired attitude. We are also interested in the level of the control signals. All physical processes have limits on the range of the control signals, so we must verify that a control program is designed not to exceed that range.

We combine the plant state vector $\underline{x}$ and the control signal vector $\underline{u}$ into a process deviation vector

$$\underline{e} = \begin{bmatrix} \underline{x} \\ \underline{u} \end{bmatrix} \tag{2.1}$$

The components of the deviation vector in which we are interested are expressed as certain linear combinations

$$q_1 = \underline{f}_1^T \underline{e}$$

$$q_2 = \underline{f}_2^T \underline{e} \tag{2.2}$$

$$\vdots$$

$$\text{etc.}$$

For example, the last control signal would be identified as

$$q_u = [\ \underline{0}^T\ |\ 1\ ]\ \underline{e} \tag{2.3}$$

An important task for the designer of the control system is to identify just what are the quantities of interest. Furthermore, he must assign a positive weighting to each of these quantities so that an overall scalar cost may be found for the proposed design.

Given the quantities of interest and their relative weights $w_i$, the rate of increase of the scalar quadratic cost is defined as

$$\frac{d}{dt} c = \sum_i w_i\, q_i^2(t) \tag{2.4}$$

Using Eq. (2.2), which defines the quantities of interest, the rate of increase of the cost may be expressed as

$$\frac{d}{dt} c = \underline{e}^T(t) \, W_{ee} \, \underline{e}(t) \tag{2.5}$$

where we have defined

$$W_{ee} = \sum_i w_i \underline{f}_i \underline{f}_i^T \tag{2.6}$$

It is obvious that the weighting matrix $W_{ee}$ is symmetric; and with the relative weights $w_i$ positive, the matrix is also positive.

The total cost of a given control operation is defined to be

$$c = \underline{x}^T(t_f) \, Q \, \underline{x}(t_f) + \int_{t_s}^{t_f} \underline{e}^T(t) \, W_{ee} \, \underline{e}(t) \, dt \tag{2.7}$$

The terminal weighting matrix $Q$ is similar in construction to the continuous weighting matrix $W_{ee}$. Certain quantities of interest related to the terminal state are identified, are given a relative weight, and are combined into a quadratic form. However, note the control signals are not included as possible quantities of interest because they will not be defined in our formulation at the terminal time.

We will assume that the plant to be controlled can be characterized by a linear vector differential equation

$$\frac{d}{dt} \underline{x}(t) = F(t) \, \underline{x}(t) + G(t) \, \underline{u}(t) + \underline{n}(t) \tag{2.8}$$

where $\underline{n}(t)$ is a white noise vector having zero mean and a covariance

$$E \, \underline{n}(t_1) \, \underline{n}^T(t_2) = N(t_1) \, \delta(t_1 - t_2) \tag{2.9}$$

where $\delta(t_1 - t_2)$ is the Dirac delta function (the impulse function). The purpose of including a possible white noise driving the state is to give the design engineer the ability to model the actual disturbances affecting the plant. One never observes a pure white noise in practice. However, often there exist noises having bandwidths broader than the bandwidth of the plant. Such noises are accurately modeled by a theoretical white noise, provided one matches the low-frequency power spectral density of the actual broad-band noise with an equal level for the white noise. In other cases a disturbance can be modeled as the output of a linear system excited by white noise. In this case one includes the linear system as part of the plant description, and one selects the level of the white noise to give the known expected level of the finite disturbance.

The computer will sample a noisy measurement process $\underline{y}$ related to the plant state $\underline{x}$ and the measurement noise $\underline{w}$ according to

$$\underline{y}(t) = M(t)\ \underline{x}(t) + \underline{w}(t) \tag{2.10}$$

We will assume that the mathematical description of the process is organized so that the measurement noise $\underline{w}(t)$ is uncorrelated from sample to sample

$$E\ \underline{w}(t_i)\ \underline{w}^T(t_j) = 0 \quad \text{for } |t_i - t_j| \geq \Delta t \tag{2.11}$$

Further, the measurement noise $\underline{w}$ is uncorrelated with the plant disturbance white noise $\underline{n}$

$$E\ \underline{w}(t_1)\ \underline{n}^T(t_2) = 0 \tag{2.12}$$

The measurement noise is given as having zero mean and a covariance

$$E\ \underline{w}(t_i)\ \underline{w}^T(t_i) = W_i \tag{2.13}$$

Note that the noise driving the plant is modeled as an infinite (white) noise; while the noise in the sampled measurements is a finite (but still uncorrelated) noise. An appropriate value for the variance of the measurement noise is often directly suggested by some physical property of the measurement process, such as the quantization size of the analogue-to-digital conversion.

Our mathematical model for the plant permits modeling of only low-pass processes. There is no term in the measurement Eq. ( 2.10) which represents a direct feed-through from control to measurement. This is no real limitation on the kinds of problems that can be treated, and it somewhat simplifies the computations that are to follow.

We assume that the matrices F, G, and M governing the plant and measurements are accurately known. In many practical applications, this assumption

10

is false. Yet we will not discuss the design of adaptive controllers, which must estimate the uncertain parameters and must perform the control function simultaneously.

The digital computer will sample the measurement process. The control computer program, using all measurements up to and including the present measurement, computes the next value of the control vector

$$\underline{u}_i = f(\underline{y}_1, \underline{y}_2, \cdots \underline{y}_i) \tag{2.14}$$

We assume that this value is held throughout the next interval up to the next measurement sample time. That is, the continuous control signal applied to the plant is

$$\underline{u}(t) = \underline{u}_i \qquad t_i \leq t < t_{i+1} \tag{2.15}$$

Some aspects of our mathematical description of the continuous stochastic process are shown in Fig. 2.1.

## 2.3 A Sampled Characterization of the Continuous Process

The state vector $\underline{x}$ of the plant is continuous in time. The control signal vector $\underline{u}$ is piecewise constant; it is discontinuous at computation times and constant between computation times. To focus our attention on the differences between the plant state and the control signal, we partition the cost weighting matrix $W_{ee}$, as defined in Eq. (2.6), in the following way:

$$W_{ee} = \begin{bmatrix} W_{xx} & | & W_{xu} \\ \hline W_{xu}^T & | & W_{uu} \end{bmatrix} \tag{2.16}$$

Then the total cost of a given control operation as defined in Eq. (2.7) may be rewritten as

$$
\begin{aligned}
c = \underline{x}^T(t_f) \, Q \, \underline{x}(t_f) & \\
+ \int_{t_s}^{t_f} & \left[ \underline{x}^T(t) \, W_{xx} \, \underline{x}(t) + \underline{x}^T(t) \, W_{xu} \, \underline{u}(t) + \underline{u}^T(t) \, W_{xu}^T \, \underline{x}(t) + \underline{u}^T(t) \, W_{uu} \, \underline{u}(t) \right] dt
\end{aligned} \tag{2.17}
$$

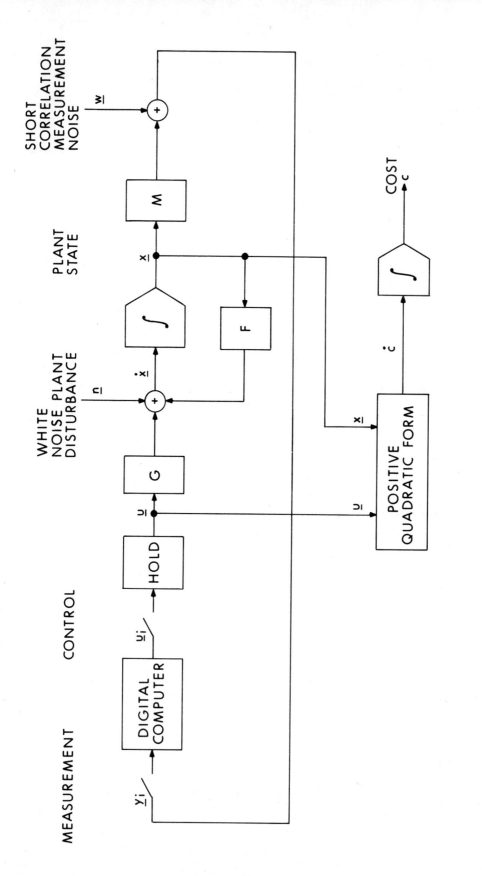

Fig. 2.1   Computer Control of a Linear Continuous Stochastic Process

The linear vector differential equation governing the plant dynamics was given by Eq. (2.8). The solution of the differential equation may be written as

$$\underline{x}(t) = A(t, t_0) \underline{x}(t_0) + \int_{t_0}^{t} A(t, \tau)[G(\tau) \underline{u}(\tau) + \underline{n}(\tau)] d\tau \tag{2.18}$$

where the state transition matrix A is defined as the solution to

$$\frac{d}{dt} A(t, t_0) = F(t) A(t, t_0) \tag{2.19}$$

subject to the initial condition

$$A(t_0, t_0) = I \tag{2.20}$$

That Eq. (2.18) is the solution to the differential equation can be verified by direct substitution into the equation. This proof is omitted.

In each interval during which the control is held piecewise constant (see Eq. (2.15)) we may write, according to Eq. (2.18),

$$\underline{x}(t) = A(t, t_i) \underline{x}_i + \int_{t_i}^{t} A(t, \tau)[G(\tau) \underline{u}_i + \underline{n}(\tau)] d\tau \tag{2.21}$$

$$\text{for } t_i \leq t < t_{i+1}$$

Or if we define the input matrix B

$$B(t, t_i) = \int_{t_i}^{t} A(t, \tau) G(\tau) d\tau \tag{2.22}$$

and the random disturbance vector $\underline{z}$

$$\underline{z}(t, t_i) = \int_{t_i}^{t} A(t, \tau) \underline{n}(\tau) d\tau \tag{2.23}$$

then the solution given in Eq. (2.21) may be rewritten

13

$$\underline{x}(t) = A(t, t_i) \, \underline{x}_i + B(t, t_i) \, \underline{u}_i + \underline{z}(t, t_i)$$

$$(2.24)$$

$$\text{for } t_i \le t < t_{i+1}$$

We will assume that the operating period of the control process, between the starting time $t_s$ and the final time $t_f$, can be neatly divided into L equal length control intervals. In this case we may rewrite the cost as given in Eq. (2.17) as

$$c = \underline{x}_{L+1}^T \, Q \underline{x}_{L+1} + \sum_{i=1}^{L} \left[ \underbrace{\int_{t_i}^{t_{i+1}} \underline{x}^T(t) \, W_{xx} \, \underline{x}(t) \, dt}_{s1_i} + \underbrace{\int_{t_i}^{t_{i+1}} \underline{x}^T(t) \, W_{xu} \, dt \, \underline{u}_i}_{s2_i} \right.$$

$$\left. + \underbrace{\underline{u}_i^T \int_{t_i}^{t_{i+1}} W_{xu}^T \, \underline{x}(t) \, dt}_{s2_i^{\ T}} + \underline{u}_i^T \int_{t_i}^{t_{i+1}} W_{uu} \, dt \, \underline{u}_i \right]$$

$$(2.25)$$

Using Eq. (2.24) the first set of integrals may be written as

$$s1_i = \int (A \, \underline{x}_i + B \, \underline{u}_i + \underline{z})^T \, W_{xx} \, (A \, \underline{x}_i + B \, \underline{u}_i + \underline{z}) \, dt \qquad (2.26)$$

which when expanded gives

$$s1_i = \underline{x}_i^T \int A^T \, W_{xx} \, A \, dt \, \underline{x}_i \quad + \quad \underline{x}_i^T \int A^T \, W_{xx} \, B \, dt \, \underline{u}_i$$

$$+ \underline{u}_i^T \int B^T \, W_{xx} \, A \, dt \, \underline{x}_i \quad + \quad \underline{u}_i^T \int B^T \, W_{xx} \, B \, dt \, \underline{u}_i$$

$$(2.27)$$

$$+ \int \underline{z}^T \, W_{xx} \, \underline{z} \, dt$$

$$+ \text{ integrals of products of } \underline{z} \text{ with } \underline{x}_i \text{ or } \underline{u}_i$$

In the second set of integrals we have

$$s2_i = \int (A \underline{x}_i + B \underline{u}_i + \underline{z})^T W_{xu} \, dt \, \underline{u}_i \qquad (2.28)$$

which when expanded gives

$$s2_i = \underline{x}_i^T \int A^T W_{xu} \, dt \, \underline{u}_i + \underline{u}_i^T \int B^T W_{xu} \, dt \, \underline{u}_i$$

$$(2.29)$$

$$+ \text{ an integral of a product of } \underline{z} \text{ with } \underline{u}_i$$

Using the expanded integrals Eqs.(2.27) and (2.29) in the cost formula Eq. (2.25) we obtain

$$c = \underline{x}_{L+1}^T Q \underline{x}_{L+1}$$

$$(2.30)$$

$$+ \sum_{i=1}^{L} \underline{x}_i^T X_i \underline{x}_i + \underline{x}_i^T S_i \underline{u}_i + \underline{u}_i^T S_i^T \underline{x}_i + \underline{u}_i^T U_i \underline{u}_i + r_i$$

where we have defined

$$X_i = \int_{t_i}^{t_{i+1}} A^T(t, t_i) W_{xx} A(t, t_i) \, dt \qquad (2.31)$$

$$S_i = \int_{t_i}^{t_{i+1}} \left[ A^T(t, t_i) W_{xx} B(t, t_i) + A^T(t, t_i) W_{xu} \right] dt \qquad (2.32)$$

$$U_i = \int_{t_i}^{t_{i+1}} \left[ B^T(t, t_i) W_{xx} B(t, t_i) + B^T(t, t_i) W_{xu} + W_{xu}^T B(t, t_i) + W_{uu} \right] dt$$

$$(2.33)$$

$$r_i = \int_{t_i}^{t_{i+1}} \underline{z}^T(t, t_i) W_{xx} \underline{z}(t, t_i) \, dt$$

$$(2.34)$$

$$+ \text{ integrals of products of } \underline{z}(t, t_i) \text{ with } \underline{x}_i \text{ or } \underline{u}_i$$

We will be evaluating control programs in a statistical sense. That is, we will want to compute the average value of the cost taken over an ensemble of operations using a given control computer program. Toward this end we examine the statistics of the noise terms. We defined the random disturbance vector $z$ in Eq. (2.23). One property of $z$ is immediately evident. Namely, since the white noise $n$ has zero mean, the disturbance $z$ also has zero mean. Further, since the white noise is assumed uncorrelated with previous values of the plant state $x_i$ or the control $u_i$, it follows that the mean values of the integrals of products of $z(t, t_i)$ with $x_i$ or $u_i$ are all zero.

We may compute the covariance of the disturbance vector $z$

$$Z(t, t_i) = E \, \underline{z}(t, t_i) \, \underline{z}(t, t_i)^T \tag{2.35}$$

Using the definition Eq. (2.23) and interchanging the order of integration and expectation gives

$$Z(t, t_i) = \int_{t_i}^{t} \int_{t_i}^{t} A(t, t_1) \, E \left[ \, \underline{n}(t_1) \, \underline{n}^T(t_2) \right] \, A^T(t, t_2) \, dt_1 \, dt_2 \tag{2.36}$$

But the autocorrelation of the white noise is given as a delta function Eq. (2.9), so this expression is reduced to

$$Z(t, t_i) = \int_{t_i}^{t} A(t, \tau) \, N(\tau) \, A^T(t, \tau) \, d\tau \tag{2.37}$$

We may calculate explicitly the mean value of the noise terms $r_i$ Eq. (2.34) in terms of the covariance $Z$ of the disturbance vector:

$$Er_i = \int_{t_i}^{t_{i+1}} E \left[ \, \underline{z}^T(t, t_i) \, W_{xx} \, \underline{z}(t, t_i) \right] \, dt \tag{2.38}$$

The quadratic form in the integrand of Eq. (2.38) is a scalar (or a one-by-one matrix). The trace of the scalar is the same as the scalar. Also the trace of the product of two rectangular matrices is unchanged if the order of the matrices is reversed. Thus we have a nonrandom formula

$$Er_i = \int_{t_i}^{t_{i+1}} \text{trace} \left[ W_{xx} \, Z(t, t_i) \right] \, dt \tag{2.39}$$

The scalar $Er_i$ has an interesting design consequence. Its value cannot be reduced by the choice of control. On the other hand, it is a function of the sample interval length $\Delta t$. An examination of this term alone might indicate that the chosen sample interval was too large, as the cost must necessarily exceed the lower bound given by

$$Ec \geq \sum_{i=1}^{L} Er_i \qquad (2.40)$$

We consider now some computational aspects in developing the sampled characterization of the continuous system. The state transition matrix A may be found directly by integrating its definition Eq. (2.19) subject to the initial condition Eq. (2.20). The input matrix B, on the other hand, is not conveniently calculated using its integral definition Eq.(2.22). It is more convenient to use the equivalent differential equation governing B. This we derive by differentiating the definition of B Eq. (2.22):

$$\frac{d}{dt} B(t, t_i) = A(t, t) G(t) + \int_{t_i}^{t} \frac{d}{dt} A(t, \tau) G(\tau) d\tau \qquad (2.41)$$

Using the properties Eqs. (2.19) and (2.20) of the state transition matrix, this reduces to

$$\frac{d}{dt} B(t, t_i) = G(t) + F(t) \int_{t_i}^{t} A(t, \tau) G(\tau) d\tau \qquad (2.42)$$

But the integral is identical to the definition of B Eq. (2.22). Thus we have found

$$\frac{d}{dt} B(t, t_i) = G(t) + F(t) B(t, t_i) \qquad (2.43)$$

In using Eq. (2.43) to compute B, it is clear from the integral definition that the initial condition must be

$$B(t_i, t_i) = 0 \qquad (2.44)$$

Another matrix not conveniently computed from its integral formulation is the covariance of the disturbance $\underline{z}$ as given by Eq. (2.37). Again we derive

17

the equivalent differential equation. In a similar manner we take the time derivative of the integral definition, we use the properties of the state transition matrix, and we identify the integral definition where it reappears. Thus we find

$$\frac{d}{dt} Z(t, t_i) = N(t) + F(t) Z(t, t_i) + Z^T(t, t_i) F^T(t) \qquad (2.45)$$

It is again clear from the integral definition that the initial condition must be

$$Z(t_i, t_i) = 0 \qquad (2.46)$$

The other matrices $X_i$, $S_i$, and $U_i$ as well as the scalar $Er_i$ can be computed directly from their formulas Eqs. (2.31), (2.32), (2.33), and (2.39).

We summarize the computations which must be encoded into a design-package computer program, which is to determine the sampled characterization of the given continuous process: We are given the time-varying matrices $F(t)$ and $G(t)$ related to the plant, the time-varying covariance matrix $N(t)$ of the plant input white noise, and the time-varying weighting matrix $W_{ee}(t)$ for the process deviation (and therefore its partitions $W_{xx}(t)$, $W_{xu}(t)$, and $W_{uu}(t)$). For each interval $i = 1$ to L we must compute $A_i$, $B_i$, $Z_i$, $X_i$, $S_i$, $U_i$, $Er_i$. The initial conditions for the i-th interval computations are

$$A = I, \ B = 0, \ Z = 0, \ X = 0, \ S = 0, \ U = 0, \ Er = 0 \qquad (2.47)$$

The differential equations to be integrated forward simultaneously from $t_i$ to $t_{i+1}$ are

$$\dot{A} = F(t) A$$
$$\dot{B} = F(t) B + G(t)$$
$$\dot{Z} = F(t) Z + Z^T F^T(t) + N(t)$$
$$\dot{X} = A^T W_{xx}(t) A$$
$$\dot{S} = A^T W_{xx}(t) B + A^T W_{xu}(t) \qquad (2.48)$$
$$\dot{U} = B^T W_{xx}(t) B + B^T W_{xu}(t) + W_{xu}^T(t) B + W_{uu}(t)$$
$$\dot{Er} = \text{trace} [W_{xx} Z]$$

The numerical integration must be repeated for each sample period. How-ever, in the special case of a constant-coefficient plant, with a stationary input white noise, and with a constant weighting matrix in the integral cost, it follows that the above equations need be integrated only for one sample period. The resulting values then hold true for all sample periods.

A helpful check on the results given by such a program is to note that for slowly varying or constant matricies, F, G, N, W and with a sample period $\Delta t$ short compared with the natural transients of the plant, the solu-tions to the differential equations are to first order given by

$$
\begin{aligned}
A &= I + F \Delta t \\
B &= G \Delta t \\
Z &= N \Delta t \\
X &= W_{xx} \Delta t \\
S &= W_{xu} \Delta t \\
U &= W_{uu} \Delta t \\
Er &= 0
\end{aligned}
\tag{2.49}
$$

Some aspects of the sampled characterization of the continuous process are shown in Fig. 2.2.

## 2.4  Computation of the Mean Quadratic Cost

We have found a sampled characterization of the continuous system. The plant state $\underline{x}$ is exactly governed by the difference equation

$$
\underline{x}_{i+1} = A_i \underline{x}_i + B_i \underline{u}_i + \underline{z}_i
\tag{2.50}
$$

where $\underline{x}_i$ is the state at the i-th sample time, $\underline{u}_i$ is the control sent out at the i-th sample time and held until the next sample time, and $\underline{z}_i$ is the net disturbance of the plant state due to white noise disturbances between the i-th sample time and the next sample time. The initial plant state is assumed to be statistically distributed with zero mean and covariance matrix

$$
E \underline{x}_1 \underline{x}_1^T = P
\tag{2.51}
$$

19

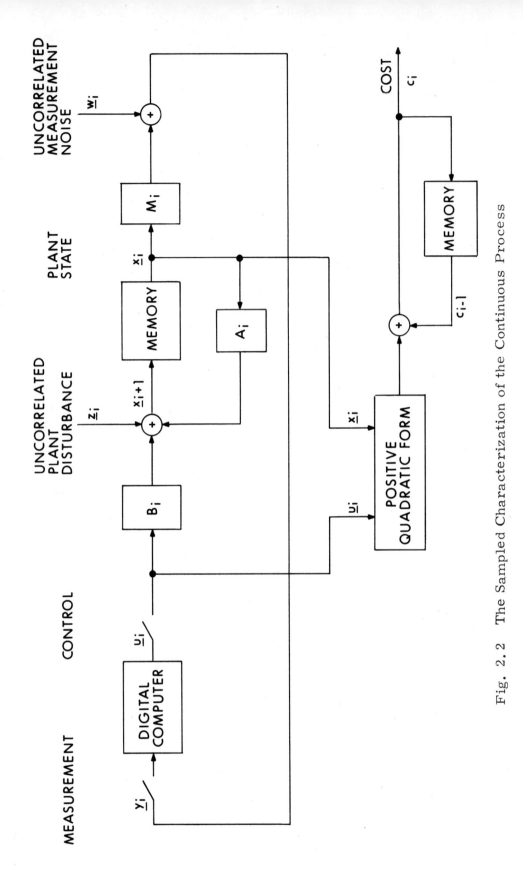

Fig. 2.2   The Sampled Characterization of the Continuous Process

20

The i-th state disturbance $z_i$ has zero mean, is uncorrelated with $x_i$, $u_i$ and all previous values of $x$ and $u$, and has covariance matrix

$$E \, z_i \, z_i^{\ T} = Z_i \tag{2.52}$$

The cost of operating the continuous process is given without approximation in a sampled form as

$$c = x_{L+1}^{\ T} \, Q \, x_{L+1}$$
$$+ \sum_{i=1}^{L} (x_i^{\ T} \, X_i \, x_i + x_i^{\ T} \, S_i \, u_i + u_i^{\ T} \, S_i^{\ T} \, x_i + u_i^{\ T} \, U_i \, u_i + r_i) \tag{2.53}$$

At the i-th sample instant the computer takes a vector measurement $y_i$

$$y_i = M_i \, x_i + w_i \tag{2.54}$$

where $w_i$ is the measurement noise which has zero mean, is uncorrelated with $x_i$ and previous values of $x$ and $u$, and has covariance matrix

$$E \, w_i \, w_i^{\ T} = W_i \tag{2.55}$$

We now introduce the specific linear control program, which takes the measurements up to and including the i-th measurement and computes the control $u_i$ to be immediately applied. If the control program is an m-th-order difference equation, we can define an m-dimensional computer state vector $v$ and can place the control program in the form

$$u_i = H_i \, v_i + C_i \, y_i \tag{2.56}$$

$$v_{i+1} = F_i \, v_i + G_i \, y_i \tag{2.57}$$

The initial computer state is assumed to be zero:

$$v_1 = 0 \tag{2.58}$$

We have chosen a form for the control computer program such that the computation of the control $\underline{u}_i$ precedes the computation of the state update, rather than a reversed form. This is the natural way that one would organize a control program. Since as a general rule lags are a destabilizing influence in a control loop, one wants to minimize the lag between taking a measurement and producing a control signal. The above choice of state space representation has the lesser computational lag.

The matrices H, F, and G in the state space representation of a given control computer program are not unique. There is an infinite variety of ways to define the state vector $\underline{v}$ such that the net transmission from measurements $\underline{y}$ to control commands $\underline{u}$ will be unchanged. We will later exploit this freedom to reduce the arithmetic required in the control computations.

As a first step in evaluating the mean cost we note that Eqs.(2.50), (2.54), (2.56), and (2.57) define a closed-loop system having no external inputs except noise. We may use Eqs.(2.54) and (2.56) to eliminate the internal variables $\underline{y}$ and $\underline{u}$ from the state formulas Eqs. (2.50) and (2.57) and from the cost formula Eq. (2.53). The resulting cost formula is

$$
c = \underline{x}_{L+1}^T Q \underline{x}_{L+1} + \sum_{i=1}^{L} \Big[ \underline{x}_i^T (X_i + S_i C_i M_i + M_i^T C_i^T S_i^T + M_i^T C_i^T U_i C_i M_i)\, \underline{x}_i
$$

$$
+ \underline{x}_i^T (S_i H_i + M_i^T C_i^T U_i H_i)\, \underline{v}_i + \underline{v}_i^T (S_i H_i + M_i^T C_i^T U_i H_i)^T\, \underline{x}_i
$$

$$
+ \underline{v}_i^T H_i^T U_i H_i \underline{v}_i + \underline{w}_i^T C_i^T U_i C_i \underline{w}_i + r_i \Big] \tag{2.59}
$$

The resulting recursive formulas governing the plant state and the computer state are

$$
\underline{x}_{i+1} = (A_i + B_i C_i M_i)\, \underline{x}_i + B_i H_i \underline{v}_i + \underline{z}_i + B_i C_i \underline{w}_i \tag{2.60}
$$

$$
\underline{v}_{i+1} = G_i M_i \underline{x}_i + F_i \underline{v}_i + G_i \underline{w}_i \tag{2.61}
$$

It is convenient to define a new state space as the direct sum of the plant state space and the computer state space. The new state vector $\underline{s}$ is

$$\underline{s}_i = \begin{bmatrix} \underline{x}_i \\ \\ \underline{v}_i \end{bmatrix} \tag{2.62}$$

We also define a new disturbance vector space as the direct sum of the plant state disturbance vector space and the measurement noise vector space. The new disturbance vector $\underline{d}$ is

$$\underline{d}_i = \begin{bmatrix} \underline{z}_i \\ \\ \underline{w}_i \end{bmatrix} \tag{2.63}$$

In terms of the state vector $\underline{s}$ and the disturbance vector $\underline{d}$ we can write the cost formula as

$$c = \underline{s}_{L+1}^T R_{L+1} \underline{s}_{L+1} + \sum_{i=1}^{L} (\underline{s}_i^T R_i \underline{s}_i + \underline{d}_i^T Y_i \underline{d}_i + r_i) \tag{2.64}$$

and we can write the recursive formula governing the state $\underline{s}$ as

$$\underline{s}_{i+1} = T_i \underline{s}_i + L_i \underline{d}_i \tag{2.65}$$

where we have defined

$$R_{L+1} = \begin{bmatrix} Q & 0 \\ \hline 0 & 0 \end{bmatrix} \tag{2.66}$$

$$R_i = \begin{bmatrix} X_i + S_i C_i M_i + M_i^T C_i^T S_i^T + M_i^T C_i^T U_i C_i M_i & S_i H_i + M_i^T C_i^T U_i H_i \\ \hline (S_i H_i + M_i^T C_i^T U_i H_i)^T & H_i^T U_i H_i \end{bmatrix} \tag{2.67}$$

$$Y_i = \begin{bmatrix} 0 & 0 \\ \hline 0 & C_i^T U_i C_i \end{bmatrix} \tag{2.68}$$

$$T_i = \begin{bmatrix} A_i + B_i C_i M_i & B_i H_i \\ \hline G_i M_i & F_i \end{bmatrix} \tag{2.69}$$

$$L_i = \begin{bmatrix} I & B_i C_i \\ \hline 0 & G_i \end{bmatrix} \tag{2.70}$$

23

By taking the expectation of the cost formula Eq. (2. 64), we have for the mean value of the cost

$$Ec = \text{trace } R_{L + 1} S_{L + 1} + \sum_{i = 1}^{L} (\text{trace } R_i S_i + \text{trace } Y_i D_i + Er_i) \qquad (2.71)$$

where we have denoted the covariance of the state and the covariance of the disturbance as

$$E \underline{s}_i \underline{s}_i^T = S_i \qquad (2.72)$$

$$E \underline{d}_i \underline{d}_i^T = D_i \qquad (2.73)$$

The covariance of the disturbance may be expressed in terms of the covariances of the plant disturbance and the measurement noise as

$$D_i = \left[ \begin{array}{c|c} Z_i & 0 \\ \hline 0 & W_i \end{array} \right] \qquad (2.74)$$

To find a recursive expression for the covariance of the state, we note from the definition Eq. (2. 72) and the recursive formula Eq. (2. 65) that

$$S_{i + 1} = E (T_i \underline{s}_i + L_i \underline{d}_i)(\underline{s}_i^T T_i^T + \underline{d}_i^T L_i^T) \qquad (2.75)$$

We expand the product and note that the disturbance $\underline{d}_i$ is not correlated with the state $\underline{s}_i$. Therefore we have

$$S_{i + 1} = T_i S_i T_i^T + L_i D_i L_i^T \qquad (2.76)$$

The initial condition to be used with this recursive formula is found by considering the definitions Eqs. (2. 72) and (2.62) together with the initial conditions Eqs. (2.51) and (2. 58). The result is

$$S_1 \triangleq \left[ \begin{array}{c|c} P & 0 \\ \hline 0 & 0 \end{array} \right] \qquad (2.77)$$

To summarize, a design-package program, which is to evaluate the mean quadratic cost of operating a given linear computer control program, must include the following steps: At the starting time of the control process define the initial covariance of the combined state $S_1$ in terms of the given initial covariance of the plant state P (Eq. (2.77)):

$$S_1 = \left[\begin{array}{c|c} P & 0 \\ \hline 0 & 0 \end{array}\right]$$

(2.78)

Also, set the partial total cost initially to zero:

$$Ec_0 = 0$$

(2.79)

For each control interval i = 1 to L sequentially compute the partial total cost $Ec_i$ and the next covariance of the combined state $S_{i+1}$ according to the recursion formulas. That is for each i:

    1. Receive from another program the sampled characterization of the continuous system including the plant-state transition matrix A, the control to state matrix B, the state to measurement matrix M, the cost sample weight matrices X, S, U, the covariance of the net interval plant disturbance Z, the covariance of the measurement noise W, and mean irreducible cost Er due to the interval disturbances. Also we receive a state space representation of the control computer program including the program state transition matrix F, the measurement to program-state matrix G, the program-state to control matrix H, and the measurement to control matrix C.

    2. In terms of the matrices given for this interval define (Eqs. (2.67), (2.68), (2.69), (2.70), and (2.74)):

$$R = \left[\begin{array}{c|c} X + SCM + M^T C^T S^T + M^T C^T UCM & SH + M^T C^T UH \\ \hline (SH + M^T C^T UH)^T & H^T UH \end{array}\right]$$

(2.80)

$$Y = \left[\begin{array}{c|c} 0 & 0 \\ \hline 0 & C^T UC \end{array}\right]$$

(2.81)

$$T = \left[\begin{array}{c|c} A + BCM & BH \\ \hline GM & F \end{array}\right]$$

(2.82)

$$L = \left[\begin{array}{c|c} I & BC \\ \hline 0 & G \end{array}\right]$$

(2.83)

$$D = \begin{bmatrix} Z & | & 0 \\ \hline 0 & | & W \end{bmatrix} \tag{2.84}$$

3.  Compute the partial total cost up to and including the present interval Eq. (2.71):

$$Ec_i = Ec_{i-1} + \text{trace } R\,S_i + \text{trace } Y\,D + Er \tag{2.85}$$

4.  Compute the next value for the covariance of the combined state Eq. (2.76):

$$S_{i+1} = T\,S_i\,T^T + L\,D\,L^T \tag{2.86}$$

After the last control interval, define the cost weighting matrix for the combined state in terms of the given terminal weighting matrix for the plant state Q Eq. (2.66):

$$R_{L+1} = \begin{bmatrix} Q & | & 0 \\ \hline 0 & | & 0 \end{bmatrix} \tag{2.87}$$

Evaluate the total mean cost, which includes the terminal cost Eq. (2.71):

$$Ec = Ec_L + \text{trace } R_{L+1}\,S_{L+1} \tag{2.88}$$

## 2.5 Computation of the Time Histories of the Mean-Squared Values of the Quantities of Interest

In some applications the single scalar cost, found by a mean-cost evaluation program, is adequate information upon which to base a next step in the design process. But in other applications the scalar cost does not convey enough information about the performance of the trial design. In these cases, the designer wishes to examine the individual quantities of interest which contribute to the cost. For example, the designer may wish to see displayed the mean-squared attitude deviation and the mean-squared control signal, both as a function of time. He may then decide that his original choice of relative weighting is not appropriate. We will be considering automatic design packages which can converge to a design which minimizes the mean scalar quadratic cost. The adequacy of the original cost statement

26

can be checked only after the minimum cost design is found and then examined in detail in terms of the individual quantities of interest.

Assume we have, from the mean-cost evaluation program, the covariance of the combined plant state and computer state at the sampling instants ($S_1$ through $S_L$) and at the terminal instant ($S_{L+1}$). In many applications we will not be interested in the magnitudes of variables internal to the control computer. In these cases, we can reduce the data first to the covariance of the process deviation vector. The deviation vector is given in terms of the state vector as

$$
\begin{bmatrix} x_i \\ \hline u_i \end{bmatrix} = \left[ \begin{array}{c|c} I & 0 \\ \hline C_i\, M_i & H_i \end{array} \right] \begin{bmatrix} x_i \\ \hline v_i \end{bmatrix} + \begin{bmatrix} 0 \\ \hline C_i \end{bmatrix} w_i \tag{2.89}
$$

(refer to Eqs. (2.54) and (2.56)). If we define the following matrices

$$
J_i = \left[ \begin{array}{c|c} I & 0 \\ \hline C_i\, M_i & H_i \end{array} \right] \tag{2.90}
$$

$$
K_i = \left[ \begin{array}{c} 0 \\ \hline C_i \end{array} \right] \tag{2.91}
$$

then the covariance of the process deviation $E_i$ can be shown to be

$$
E_i = J_i\, S_i\, J_i^{\,T} + K_i\, W_i\, K_i^{\,T} \tag{2.92}
$$

where $W_i$ is the covariance of the measurement noise.

To interpolate between sample instants we note that the deviation vector is governed by the differential equation

$$
\begin{bmatrix} \dot{x} \\ \hline \dot{u} \end{bmatrix} = \left[ \begin{array}{c|c} F & G \\ \hline 0 & 0 \end{array} \right] \begin{bmatrix} x \\ \hline u \end{bmatrix} + \begin{bmatrix} I \\ \hline 0 \end{bmatrix} n \tag{2.93}
$$

except of course at the sample instants when the control has a step discontinuity. If we define the following matrices

$$H = \left[ \begin{array}{c|c} F & G \\ \hline 0 & 0 \end{array} \right] \qquad (2.94)$$

$$D = \left[ \begin{array}{c} I \\ \hline 0 \end{array} \right] \qquad (2.95)$$

then it can be shown that between sample instants the deviation vector is given by

$$\underline{e}(t) = C(t, t_i) \underline{e}_i + \int_{t_i}^{t} C(t, \tau) D \underline{n}(\tau) d\tau \qquad (2.96)$$

where C is the solution to

$$\frac{d}{dt} C(t, t_i) = H(t) C(t, t_i) \qquad (2.97)$$

subject to the initial condition

$$C(t_i, t_i) = I \qquad (2.98)$$

Using Eq.(2.96) it can be shown that between sample instants the covariance of the deviation vector is given by

$$E(t) = C(t, t_i) E_i C^T(t, t_i)$$
$$+ \int_{t_i}^{t} C(t, \tau) D N(\tau) D^T C^T(t, \tau) d\tau \qquad (2.99)$$

where N is the covariance of the plant input white noise. For computation, the equivalent differential equation is more convenient. This is found by taking the time derivative of Eq.(2.99), by using the properties of C Eqs. (2.97) and (2.98), and by identifying the integral representation of E when it reappears. The result is

$$\frac{d}{dt} E(t) = H(t) E(t) + E^T(t) H^T(t) + D N(t) D^T \qquad (2.100)$$

subject to the initial condition

$$E(t_i) = E_i \qquad (2.101)$$

Having found the time variation of the covariance of the process deviation between sample instants, the time variation of the individual quantities of interest follows immediately. If we are interested in the quantity $q_1$,

$$q_1(t) = \underline{f}_1^T \, \underline{e}(t) \tag{2.102}$$

then the mean-square value of $q_1$ is given by

$$E[q_1^2(t)] = \underline{f}_1^T \, E(t) \, \underline{f}_1 \tag{2.103}$$

To summarize, a design-package program, which is to compute the time histories of the mean-squared values of the quantities of interest, must include the following steps:

1. At the beginning of each control interval ($i = 1$ to $L$) the covariance $S_i$ of the combined plant and computer state space is received from another program.

2. Reduce the data to the covariance $E_i$ of the process deviation (plant state plus control vector) by calculating (Eqs. (2.90), (2.91), (2.92))

$$J = \begin{bmatrix} I & 0 \\ \hline CM & H \end{bmatrix} \tag{2.104}$$

$$K = \begin{bmatrix} 0 \\ \hline C \end{bmatrix} \tag{2.105}$$

$$E_i = J \, S_i \, J^T + K \, W \, K^T \tag{2.106}$$

3. Compute the covariance $E(t)$ between $t_i$ and the next sample instant $t_{i+1}$ by integrating the differential equation (Eqs. (2.94), (2.95), (2.100)):

$$H(t) = \begin{bmatrix} F(t) & G(t) \\ \hline 0 & 0 \end{bmatrix} \tag{2.107}$$

$$D = \begin{bmatrix} I \\ \hline 0 \end{bmatrix} \tag{2.108}$$

29

$$\frac{d}{dt} E(t) = H(t) E(t) + E^T(t) H^T(t) + DN(t) D^T \tag{2.109}$$

subject to the initial condition (Eq. (2.101))

$$E(t_i) = E_i \tag{2.110}$$

During the integration, the mean-square value of the $j$-th quantity of interest is computed from the auxiliary relation (Eq. (2.103)):

$$MS\, q_j(t) = \underline{f}_j^T\, E(t)\, \underline{f}_j \tag{2.111}$$

## 2.6 An Evaluation of the Short Burn Performance of a Spacecraft Steering Law

A guidance scheme used in many phases of powered flight in the Apollo mission is called cross-product steering (see Copps (1964)). A velocity-to-be-gained is defined as the difference between the required velocity and the present velocity of the spacecraft (see Fig. 2.3). If the current acceleration of the spacecraft is not aligned with the velocity-to-be-gained, a rotational command is sent to the attitude control autopilot according to the cross product of $\underline{a}$ and $\underline{v}_g$

$$\underline{\omega}_{cmd} = K\, \frac{\underline{a} \times \underline{v}_g}{|\underline{a}|\, |\underline{v}_g|} \tag{2.112}$$

More refined steer laws are generally used (again see Copps), but the above law is adequate for our present discussion.

In the on-board guidance computer the continuous steer law is approximated by a sampled version.

$$\Delta \underline{v}_i = \underline{v}_i - \underline{v}_{i-1}$$

$$\Delta \underline{\theta}c_i = K_i\, \frac{\Delta \underline{v}_i \times \underline{v}g_i}{|\Delta \underline{v}_i|\, |\underline{v}g_i|}\, \Delta t \tag{2.113}$$

That is, the present acceleration is estimated from a back difference of readings from the integrating accelerometers. Upon calculation of the cross product an increment to the commanded attitude is sent to the attitude control autopilot. The autopilot attempts to reach the commanded attitude, which is held until the next computation time.

In a design currently being considered for Apollo, the sampling interval is $\Delta t = 2$ sec. and the steer-law gain is $K = .1$. With this low gain the sampled-data version closely follows the behavior of the continuous control law. Far removed from the cut-off time, the inertial direction of $v_g$ remains essentially constant; the steer law brings the vehicle acceleration into alignment with the $v_g$ vector, as a first-order system with a time constant $1/K$ (10 sec. for $K = .1$). The advantage of a low gain is the greater stability, the lower sensitivity to noise, and the lower demands on the attitude control autopilot. The disadvantage of a low gain is that there will be a large velocity cut-off error for a short duration burn (a burn of the order of the steer-law time constant). The steer law is not sufficiently fast to rotate the acceleration into the velocity-to-be-gained, within the remaining time-to-go.

In this chapter we have developed a systematic sequence of computations for evaluating linear control programs. The evaluation of the cross-product steer law is a good illustration of these general techniques. The mathematical model for the vehicle and the attitude control autopilot is discussed in Appendix A. A fifth-order model for the plant is shown to be

$$\frac{d}{dt}\begin{bmatrix} \epsilon \\ v_{\perp} \\ \omega \\ \theta \\ r \end{bmatrix} = \begin{bmatrix} 0 & 0 & 0 & 0 & 0 \\ 0 & 0 & 0 & 22 & -10 \\ -1.13 & 0 & 0 & -1.36 & 1.13 \\ 0 & 0 & 1 & 0 & 0 \\ 0 & 0 & 0 & 2.16 & -2 \end{bmatrix} \begin{bmatrix} \epsilon \\ v_{\perp} \\ \omega \\ \theta \\ r \end{bmatrix} + \begin{bmatrix} 0 \\ -12 \\ 1.36 \\ 0 \\ -2.16 \end{bmatrix} \theta_c \qquad (2.114)$$

$$v_a = \begin{bmatrix} 0 & 1 & 0 & 0 & 0 \end{bmatrix} \begin{bmatrix} \epsilon \\ v_{\perp} \\ \omega \\ \theta \\ r \end{bmatrix} + w_v \qquad (2.115)$$

where $\epsilon$ is the angular offset of the center-of-mass of the vehicle (angle away from the centerline as seen from the engine gimbal station), $v_{\perp}$ is the unwanted component of velocity of the center-of-mass of the vehicle (perpendicular to the initial required velocity), $\omega$ is the angular velocity of the vehicle, $\theta$ is the inertial attitude of the centerline of the vehicle relative to the direction of the initial required velocity, and r is a state variable modeling the low-frequency characteristics of the attitude control autopilot cascaded with the engine nozzle-angle actuator. The nozzle angle $\delta$ cannot appear as a state variable in this representation, because it contains a high pass term directly proportional to the control signal $\theta_c$.

Three quantities are of particular interest in this problem: the unwanted lateral velocity $v_\perp$, the angular velocity of the vehicle $\omega$ and the nozzle activity as measured by its deviation away from the angular location of the center-of-mass ($\delta - \epsilon$). The quantities of interest can be expressed as linear combinations of the state variables and the control signal $\theta_c$. (For the nozzle angle linear combination see Eq. (A-17).)

$$
\begin{bmatrix} v_\perp \\ \omega \\ \delta - \epsilon \end{bmatrix} = \begin{bmatrix} 0 & 1 & 0 & 0 & 0 & 0 \\ 0 & 0 & 1 & 0 & 0 & 0 \\ -1 & 0 & 0 & -1.2 & 1 & 1.2 \end{bmatrix} \begin{bmatrix} \epsilon \\ v_\perp \\ \omega \\ \theta \\ r \\ \theta_c \end{bmatrix} \tag{2.116}
$$

The three quantities of interest all must be considered in evaluating the performance of a given steer law. The basic control objective is to reduce the unwanted component of velocity $v_\perp$ to zero at cut-off. In addition the vehicle should reach cut-off with zero angular velocity, or else attitude control jets will have to waste fuel to arrest the tumbling. However, unlimited control action cannot be called for to achieve these terminal objectives; the physical nozzle is only free to travel between plus and minus 5 degrees.

A quadratic cost formula which penalizes these three quantities is

$$
\text{cost} = \left[ \frac{1}{2} M v_\perp^2 + \frac{1}{2} I \omega^2 \right]_{t=T} + \int_0^T w (\delta - \epsilon)^2 dt \tag{2.117}
$$

The velocity error and rotation rate at cut-off have been weighted equally according to their kinetic energies. The nozzle penalty will be added with a weight of $w = 10^6$. This value for nozzle weight has not been pulled out of the air. Rather we have designed and evaluated an optimal steering-control computer program according to the theory reviewed in the next chapter. A weight of $w = 10^6$ leads to an optimal design having a peak RMS nozzle angle of 2.7 degrees, which is an acceptable nozzle activity. It seems reasonable to compare other nonoptimal designs, such as our present example, using the same components in the scalar cost formula.

The cost formula in this example illustrates the general type introduced in Eq. (2.7). It includes a penalty on joint state and control. In the general form, the process deviation weighting matrix of Eq. (2.6) is

$$W_{ee} = \begin{bmatrix} 1 & 0 & 0 & 1.2 & -1 & -1.2 \\ 0 & 0 & 0 & 0 & 0 & 0 \\ 0 & 0 & 0 & 0 & 0 & 0 \\ 1.2 & 0 & 0 & 1.44 & -1.2 & -1.44 \\ -1 & 0 & 0 & -1.2 & 1 & 1.2 \\ -1.2 & 0 & 0 & -1.44 & 1.2 & 1.44 \end{bmatrix} \times 10^6 \qquad (2.118)$$

The terminal state weighting matrix is

$$Q = \begin{bmatrix} 0 & 0 & 0 & 0 & 0 \\ 0 & 1100 & 0 & 0 & 0 \\ 0 & 0 & 185000 & 0 & 0 \\ 0 & 0 & 0 & 0 & 0 \\ 0 & 0 & 0 & 0 & 0 \end{bmatrix} \qquad (2.119)$$

The sampled characterization of the continuous process may be computed by the procedure summarized at the end of Sec. 2.3 (see Eqs. (2.47) and (2.48)). As a result we find the state transition representation of the plant to be

$$\begin{bmatrix} \epsilon \\ v_1 \\ \omega \\ \theta \\ r \end{bmatrix}_{i+1} = \begin{bmatrix} 1 & 0 & 0 & 0 & 0 \\ -20.5 & 1 & 22.9 & 15.6 & 3.98 \\ -1.39 & 0 & .149 & -.380 & .198 \\ -1.74 & 0 & 1.23 & .149 & .595 \\ -1.24 & 0 & 1.14 & .379 & .512 \end{bmatrix} \begin{bmatrix} \epsilon \\ v_1 \\ \omega \\ \theta \\ r \end{bmatrix}_i + \begin{bmatrix} 0 \\ 4.35 \\ .380 \\ .851 \\ -.379 \end{bmatrix} \theta c_i$$

$$\qquad (2.120)$$

33

The sampled formulation of the continuous cost is found to be

$$\text{cost} = \underline{x}_{L+1}^T \; Q \; \underline{x}_{L+1}$$

$$+ \sum_{i=1}^{L} (\underline{x}_i^T \; X \; \underline{x}_i + \underline{x}_i^T \; S \; \theta c_i + \theta c_i \; S^T \; \underline{x}_i + \theta c_i \; U \; \theta c_i) \qquad (2.121)$$

where

$$X = \begin{bmatrix} 902 & 0 & 433 & 397 & -267 \\ 0 & 0 & 0 & 0 & 0 \\ 433 & 0 & 309 & 55.0 & -2.79 \\ 397 & 0 & 55.0 & 362 & -291 \\ -267 & 0 & -2.79 & -291 & 239 \end{bmatrix} \times 10^3$$

$$S = \begin{bmatrix} -397 \\ 0 \\ -55.0 \\ -362 \\ 291 \end{bmatrix} \times 10^3$$

$$U = [\, 362\, ] \times 10^3$$

(The matrix Z and scalar Er, also computed by the methods of Sec. 2.3, are zero; because we have assumed in this example that there is no noise driving the plant state.)

Many contributors in the literature suggest the approximate formulas (Eq. (2.49)) give an appropriate conversion of the continuous process into a sampled form. Note, however, in our example how poor these approximate formulas would be, because the steering loop sample interval of $\Delta t = 2$ sec. is not short compared with the attitude control response time.

To illustrate the basic control problem, we can evaluate the performance of the spacecraft if there is no steer law active in the guidance computer. Using the techniques of Secs. 2.4 and 2.5 we can compute the time histories of the mean-squared values of the vehicle attitude and lateral velocity, if the

34

attitude command is held constant at zero. The results are shown in Fig. 2.4. Due to the center-of-mass uncertainty of 1 degree RMS, the vehicle swings out to a steady-state attitude error of 8 degrees RMS in order that the attitude control autopilot, with its low-frequency gain of 1/8, can hold the nozzle at the required angle through the center-of-mass. With this large heading error, the vehicle picks up an unwanted component of velocity perpendicular to the required velocity. This lateral velocity continues to grow and results in a cut-off error of 30 ft/sec. RMS in a 20-sec. burn.

The guidance computer steer law was given in Eq. (2.113). We can linearize the steer law if we assume that the acceleration vector never swings far away from the direction of the required velocity. Then consistent with small angle approximations we have

$$\Delta v_{a_i} = v_{a_i} - v_{a_{i-1}}$$

$$\alpha_i = -\frac{1}{a\,T_{go_i}}\, v_{a_i} - \frac{1}{a\,\Delta t}\,\Delta v_{a_i} \qquad (2.122)$$

$$\theta c_i = \theta c_{i-1} + K_i\,\alpha_i\,\Delta t$$

The first calculation in set (2.122) is an estimate of the change in lateral velocity based upon the measurements $v_{a_i}$. The second formula computes the angle between the velocity-to-be-gained vector and the estimated acceleration vector. The last formula computes the attitude command signal $\theta c_i$.

For a state space representation of the linearized control program, we eliminate the intermediate variables $\Delta v_a$ and $\alpha$, and we define a state variable x. The resulting first-order state space representation is

$$\theta c_i = [1]\,x_i + c_i\,v_{a_i} \qquad (2.123)$$

$$x_{i+1} = [1]\,x_i + g_i\,v_{a_i}$$

where

$$c_i = -\frac{K_i}{a}\left(\frac{\Delta t}{T_{go_i}} + 1\right)$$

$$g_i = -\frac{K_i}{a}\left(\frac{\Delta t}{T_{go_i}} + 1\right) + \frac{K_{i+1}}{a}$$

35

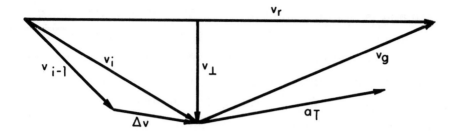

Fig. 2.3    Vectors which Occur in the Steering Problem

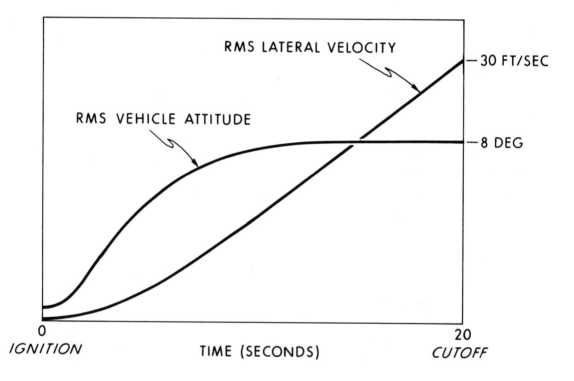

Fig. 2.4    With No Steering, the Vehicle Attitude Error Leads
to a Large-Velocity Error at Cut-off

36

This is a linear time-varying control program; the coefficients are a function of the time-to-go. We may also wish to use a nonconstant sequence for the steer-law gains $K_i$.

Given the sampled characterization for the continuous plant and cost function, and given the state space representation for the steer law, we now can compute the mean cost related to this steer law as well as the sequence of covariances of the combined plant and steer-law state. The required computations were summarized at the end of Sec. 2.4 (Eqs. (2.78) through (2.88)). The mean total cost, for a 20-sec. burn with a steer-law gain of $K = .1$ and a sample interval of $\Delta t = 2$ sec., is

$$Ec = 55,000 \text{ ft.-lb.}$$

(This includes both the terminal energy and the weighted nozzle deviation).

Given the sequence of covariances of the combined plant and steer-law state, we can compute the time histories of the mean-squared values of the quantities of interest. The required computations were summarized at the end of Sec. 2.5 (Eqs. (2.104) through (2.111)). The RMS values of the lateral velocity $v_\perp$, the vehicle rotation rate $\omega$, and the nozzle deviation $\delta - \epsilon$ are shown in Fig. 2.5. The steer law acts to bring the unwanted component of velocity back toward zero. However, due to the low steer-law gain together with the short burn duration, there is a substantial velocity error at cut-off. Also the angle of the velocity to-be-gained vector accelerates away from the vehicle near cut-off, causing increasingly large increments to commanded attitude. This causes an acceptably high vehicle rotation rate at cut-off.

An engineering solution to this problem is to suppress the steering equations for the last computation instant and continue to hold the last commanded attitude until cut-off. We can evaluate this idea by setting the steer-law gain to zero in the last computation (set $K_L = 0$) and by repeating the evaluation procedure. The relative performance with and without the last command suppressed is also seen in Fig. 2.5. Introducing the attitude hold has successfully reduced the angular velocity at cut-off to an acceptable value at the cost of a slight increase in cut-off velocity error.

It is common in the literature concerning sampled-data systems to consider the behavior of the control system only at the sampling instants. Had we used such an approach in this example, we would not have learned of the

37

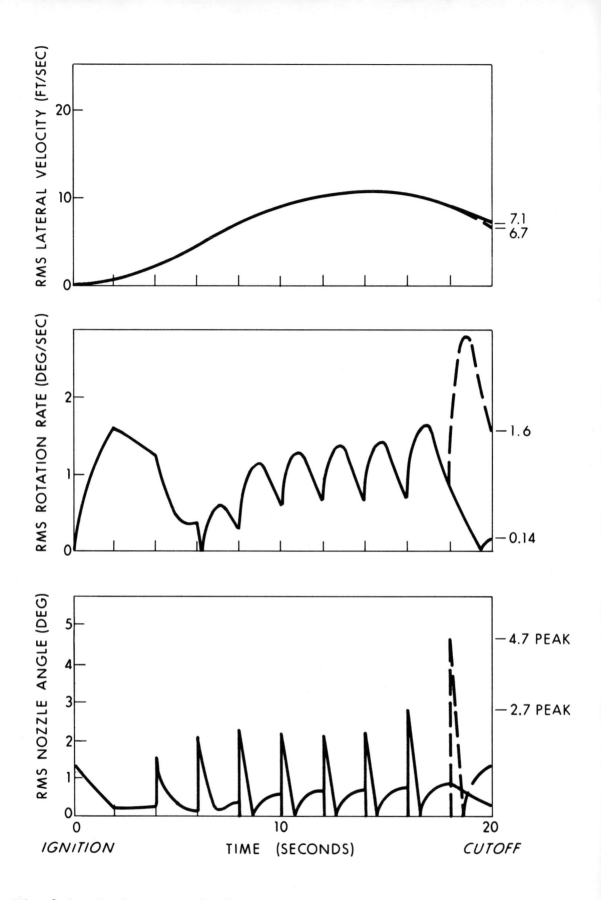

Fig. 2.5    Performance of a Cross-Product Steer Law with K = .1 and Δt =2 sec.

38

highly transient nature of the nozzle activity or of the vehicle rotation rate. With the additional information between sample instants, the designer is motivated to seek solutions to this steering problem which exhibit smoother operation. If computer capacity permits a more frequent computation of the steering law, then such a sample-interval reduction could smooth the operation. According to Eq. (2.113), for a given steer-law gain, reducing the sample-interval $\Delta t$ would reduce the size of the increments to the attitude control autopilot, thereby reducing the size of the nozzle excursions. This suggested design change has been evaluated, again using the techniques of this chapter. The change does improve the smoothness of the steering operation.

An alternate suggestion would be to incorporate a higher-order hold for the attitude control signal. Instead of introducing a step discontinuity into the attitude command (a zero-order hold) one could consider the output of the steering law to be the desired angular velocity $\underline{\omega}_{cmd}$ (see Eq. (2.112)). The attitude control loop would construct a continuous attitude $\theta_c$ by integrating the $\omega_{cmd}$ currently being held.

# Chapter 3
## Synthesis of Optimal Measurement-Limited Linear
### Sampled-Data Controllers

## 3.1 Introduction

The mathematical description of the continuous stochastic process was presented in Chapter 2. It was shown how the continuous formulation could be converted into a sampled-data formulation. Then given any linear computer control program, it was shown how to evaluate the performance of that program in the stochastic environment.

A very elegant theory has been developed for designing sampled-data controllers which exhibit optimal performance. In this chapter the theory is reviewed, and then practical implementations of the indicated control computer programs are discussed. Given a certain sample interval $\Delta t$, one is able to design explicitly a control computer program which will take the available measurements and produce appropriate control signals. By appropriate control signals, one means that the controller will minimize the given quadratic cost function averaged over an ensemble of operations of the process. This is the minimum-cost <u>linear</u> program for controlling the assumed linear plant. If the disturbances happen to be Gaussian, then in addition one can say that no nonlinear controller can do any better.

It is often the case with computer control systems that the measurement sampling rate is not fixed by the sensors or by the computer design itself, but rather it may be selected by the control computer program designer. In this case one must re-examine the significance of the optimal control theory. The so-called optimal control program is optimal in the sense that <u>at that sample-rate</u> no other program can do better. Yet in general if one can reduce the size of the sampling interval, it is possible to provide tighter control with a resulting reduction in the performance cost. If one had an infinitely fast control computer, one could obtain the best performance by simulating the optimal continuous controller. However, the designer is not free to specify the speed at which the computer must perform the arithmetic required

41

by a control program. Usually the design of the control computer is fixed in advance. It falls on the control system engineer as a final step to find the best _program_ for the given computer and plant. Since the arithmetic speed is fixed, the designer can obtain a reduction in the sampling period only if he reduces the number of calculations which must be performed each sample period. It is quite likely that there exist control programs, simpler than an "optimal" control program, which because of their faster sampling rates achieve better performance. This possibility is discussed by Robinson ( 1957 ). He refers to the problem which has been solved in the literature as the data-limited (or measurement-limited) optimal design problem. The other problem, which is largely unsolved, he calls the computer-limited optimal design problem.

It is not generally realized that the optimal measurement-limited controller is not unique. Joseph and Tou (1961) proved that the cascade of a minimum variance estimator of the plant state with an optimum deterministic controller is _a_ design which minimizes the cost. However, there are many other designs which also minimize the cost. Having found the Joseph and Tou cascade synthesis, there is nothing sacred about the internal state vector of the controller. There is an infinite family of transformations of the controller state space which leave the net transmission from measurements to control signals unchanged. Thus, one is free to find state space representations for the Joseph and Tou synthesis which minimize the required arithmetic and thus permit a faster choice for the sampling rate. In Sec. 3. 3 we discuss alternate canonical forms which meet this objective.

In Sec. 3. 4 we synthesize an optimal control computer program for an air-to-air missile. This program is transformed into a standard form requiring only seven time-varying coefficients and seven multiplications in each computation cycle.

## 3. 2   Review of Optimal Sampled-Data Control Theory

Consider first the deterministic nonstochastic control problem. The object is to minimize the cost as given by

$$c = \underline{x}_{L+1}^T \, Q_{L+1} \, \underline{x}_{L+1} + \sum_{i=1}^{L} \underline{x}_i^T \, X_i \, \underline{x}_i + \underline{x}_i^T \, S_i \, \underline{u}_i + \underline{u}_i^T \, S_i^T \, \underline{x}_i + \underline{u}_i^T \, U_i \, \underline{u}_i$$

(3. 1)

The transitions of the state of the plant are governed by

$$\underline{x}_{i+1} = A_i \, \underline{x}_i + B_i \, \underline{u}_i \qquad (3.2)$$

There is no disturbance driving the plant state. Also we assume that all the components of the state vector are measurable without error by the control computer.

This problem was solved by Kalman and Koepcke (1958). The optimal control signal, to be held constant during the next control interval, is a linear memoryless (but time-varying) function of the state measured at the beginning of the control interval.

$$\underline{u}_i = - C_i \, \underline{x}_i \qquad (3.3)$$

At any of the sampling times $t_i$ the value of the minimum cost of completing the control operation ($t_i$ to $t_{L+1}$) is a quadratic function of the present state.

$$\min c_i = \underline{x}_i^T \, Q_i \, \underline{x}_i \qquad (3.4)$$

The computation of the sequence of optimal gains $C_i$ is a task easily programmed on a general-purpose digital computer. Starting at the terminal time with the terminal cost weighting matrix $Q_{L+1}$ as given in Eq. (3.1), the optimal gains $C_i$ and the minimum cost matrices $Q_i$ are computed recursively backwards from $i = L$ to $i = 1$:

$$C_i = (B_i^T \, Q_{i+1} \, B_i + U_i)^{-1} \, (B_i^T \, Q_{i+1} \, A_i + S_i^T) \qquad (3.5)$$

$$Q_i = (A_i - B_i \, C_i)^T \, Q_{i+1} \, (A_i - B_i \, C_i)$$

$$+ \, C_i^T \, U_i \, C_i - C_i^T \, S_i^T - S_i \, C_i + X_i \qquad (3.6)$$

The recursive formulas Eqs. (3.5) and (3.6) differ somewhat from the formulas derived by Kalman and Koepcke. We have extended their result to include the possibility that the control is vector valued rather than just a scalar. Also we have organized the recursive formula for the minimum cost matrix $Q_i$ Eq. (3.6) so that it is in a symmetrical form, less sensitive

43

to computational difficulties. These difficulties are analogous to the computational difficulties encountered in the design of optimal estimators, which will be discussed later.

Now in general all the components of the plant state vector are not directly accessible to the digital controller. Therefore, to implement a control law analogous to Eq. (3.3) one must first generate estimates of all the state components based upon the noisy measurements that are available. Kalman (1960) showed how to construct the linear estimator which would minimize simultaneously the mean-squared errors in each component of the estimate. In the stochastic problem the measurements $\underline{y}_i$ and the plant state $\underline{x}_i$ are governed by

$$\underline{y}_i = M_i \, \underline{x}_i + \underline{w}_i \qquad (3.7)$$

$$\underline{x}_{i+1} = A_i \, \underline{x}_i + B_i \, \underline{u}_i + \underline{z}_i \qquad (3.8)$$

The initial plant state $\underline{x}_1$, the sequence of measurement noises $\underline{w}_i$, and the sequence of plant-state disturbances $\underline{z}_i$ are random vectors with first-and second-order statistics known to be

$$E \, \underline{w}_i = \underline{0} \qquad (3.9)$$

$$E \, \underline{z}_i = \underline{0} \qquad (3.10)$$

$$E \, \underline{x}_1 = \underline{0} \qquad (3.11)$$

$$E \, \underline{w}_i \, \underline{w}_j^T = W_i \, \delta_{ij} \qquad (3.12)$$

$$E \, \underline{z}_i \, \underline{z}_j^T = Z_i \, \delta_{ij} \qquad (3.13)$$

$$E \, \underline{x}_1 \, \underline{x}_1^T = P_1 \qquad (3.14)$$

$$E \, \underline{w}_i \, \underline{z}_j^T = 0 \qquad (3.15)$$

$$E \, \underline{x}_1 \, \underline{w}_i^T = 0 \qquad (3.16)$$

$$E \, \underline{x}_1 \, \underline{z}_i^T = 0 \qquad (3.17)$$

where $\delta_{ij}$ is unity if i=j and is zero otherwise. The linear estimator having minimum mean-squared error has the following structure:

$$\hat{\underline{x}} \, (t_i \mid i) = \hat{\underline{x}} \, (t_i \mid i-1) + K_i \, [\underline{y}_i - M_i \, \hat{\underline{x}} \, (t_i \mid i-1)] \qquad (3.18)$$

$$\hat{\underline{x}} \, (t_{i+1} \mid i) = A_i \, \hat{\underline{x}} \, (t_i \mid i) + B_i \, \underline{u}_i \qquad (3.19)$$

for i = 1 to L. The initial estimate is

$$\hat{\underline{x}} \, (t_1 \mid 0) = \underline{0} \qquad (3.20)$$

That is, the best estimate of the state at time $t_1$ given 0 measurements is the zero vector (the initial state has zero mean). After taking the measurement $\underline{y}_i$, the best estimate of the state at time $t_i$ given all i measurements is equal to the best estimate before the i-th measurement plus a weighting matrix $K_i$ times the difference between the actual measurement and the expected measurement. The best extrapolation of the best estimate after the measurement is according to the state transition matrix of the plant as driven by the known control signal being applied during this interval.

Define $P_i$ to be the covariance matrix of the error in the optimal state estimate at time $t_i$ but before the i-th measurement:

$$P_i = E \, [\hat{\underline{x}} \, (t_i \mid i - 1) - \underline{x}_i] \, [\hat{\underline{x}} \, (t_i \mid i - 1) - \underline{x}_i]^T \qquad (3.21)$$

The sequence of optimal weighting matrices $K_i$ and the sequence of optimal error matrices $P_i$ can be computed recursively forward from i = 1 to i = L:

$$K_i = P_i \, M_i^T \, (M_i \, P_i \, M_i^T + W_i)^{-1} \qquad (3.22)$$

$$P_{i+1} = A_i \, [(I - K_i \, M_i) \, P_i \, (I - K_i \, M_i)^T + K_i \, W_i \, K_i^T] \, A_i^T + Z_i \qquad (3.23)$$

The initial value $P_1$ for the estimation error matrix is identical to the initial covariance of the plant state Eq. (3.14).

The above formulation of the Kalman estimator is taken from course notes written by Joseph ( 1964 ). The Joseph formulation is somewhat different from that originally given by Kalman. In Joseph's formulation Eq. (3.23) the term in square brackets is the optimal error matrix after incorporating the measurement, but before extrapolation

$$\overline{P} = (I - K \, M) \, P \, (I - K \, M)^T + K \, W \, K^T \qquad (3.24)$$

45

It can be shown that Eq. (3.24) is algebraically equivalent to

$$\overline{P} = (I - KM) P \qquad (3.25)$$

provided the matrix K is the optimal matrix, as computed by Eq. (3.22). This shorter formula Eq. (3.25) has often been suggested in the literature. Joseph points out, however, that this is not a desirable simplification. He considers the possibility that the calculated optimal gains are in error by $\delta K$. Then, assuming perfect precision in computing Eq. (3.25), the error matrix will be incorrect by an amount

$$\delta \overline{P} = -\delta K M P \qquad (3.26)$$

In this unbalanced formulation, a first-order error in the matrix K produces a first-order error in the matrix $\overline{P}$. With the Joseph formulation, on the other hand, an error in the optimal gain matrix $\delta K$ would lead to an error in the estimation error matrix of

$$\delta \overline{P} = \delta K [WK^T - MP(I - KM)^T] + [KW - (I - KM)PM^T] \delta K^T \qquad (3.27)$$

If the matrix K is nominally given by Eq. (3.22), then it must satisfy

$$K(MPM^T + W) - PM^T = KW - (I - KM)PM^T = 0 \qquad (3.28)$$

Therefore to first order, the inaccuracy in the estimation error matrix caused by an inaccuracy in the gain matrix is

$$\delta \overline{P} = 0 \qquad (3.29)$$

A first-order error in K produces at most a second-order error in $\overline{P}$.

From an alternate point of view, one can consider the effect of floating-point arithmetic truncation on the accuracy of the two formulations. One often encounters a practical situation where the uncertainty P before the measurement is large but the uncertainty $\overline{P}$ after the measurement is small. In this situation K M would be nearly equal to I. But in computing Eq. (3.25) the difference between the two nearly equal arrays can have many less significant figures than have the original arrays. Then the accuracy of the result can be seriously reduced. With Joseph's formulation, on the other hand, in computing Eq. (3.24) the troublesome difference (I-KM) enters quadratically and is therefore made very small. The computed value for P is dominated by the term $KWK^T$, which involves no loss of accuracy.

A possible synthesis of a stochastic controller could include a Kalman minimum variance linear state estimator cascaded with the Kalman-Koepcke

46

minimum quadratic cost deterministic controller, operating on the state estimates as though they were actual measurements of the state. The resulting linear control computer program would be

$$\hat{\underline{x}}\,(t_i \mid i) = \hat{\underline{x}}\,(t_i \mid i - 1) + K_i\,[\underline{y}_i - M_i\,\hat{\underline{x}}\,(t_i \mid i - 1)] \tag{3.30}$$

$$\underline{u}_i = -\,C_i\,\hat{\underline{x}}\,(t_i \mid i) \tag{3.31}$$

$$\hat{\underline{x}}\,(t_{i+1} \mid i) = A_i\,\hat{\underline{x}}\,(t_i \mid i) + B_i\,\underline{u}_i \tag{3.32}$$

This sampled-data controller is illustrated in Fig. 3.1. It is not obvious
that this combination of state estimator and controller (which were designed
separately) is optimum in any overall sense. Joseph and Tou (1961)
succeeded in proving that this combination indeed is an optimal design for
the stochastic environment. It will minimize the mean value of the cost.

As a minor note, the cost given in Eq. (3.1) differs from the sampled
cost given in Eq. (2.30) in that the terms $r_i$ are omitted. However, since
the mean values of the terms $r_i$ are not a function of the choice of control,
this omission does not invalidate the Joseph and Tou optimal synthesis
theorem.

## 3.3 Minimum Arithmetic Canonical Forms for Linear Time-Varying Control Computer Programs

As a first step in reducing the number of multiplications and additions
which must be performed by the control computer, one combines Eqs. (3.30),
(3.31), and (3.32) into a simpler state space representation for the optimal
control program. Let $\hat{\underline{x}}\,(t_i \mid i - 1)$ be the basic state vector of the control
program, denoted simply $\underline{x}_i$. Eliminate the internal variable $\hat{\underline{x}}\,(t_i \mid i)$. The
resulting representation is

$$\underline{u}_i = H_i\,\underline{x}_i + D_i\,\underline{y}_i \tag{3.33}$$

$$\underline{x}_{i+1} = F_i\,\underline{x}_i + G_i\,\underline{y}_i \tag{3.34}$$

where

$$H_i = -\,C_i\,(I - K_i\,M_i) \tag{3.35}$$

$$D_i = -\,C_i\,K_i \tag{3.36}$$

47

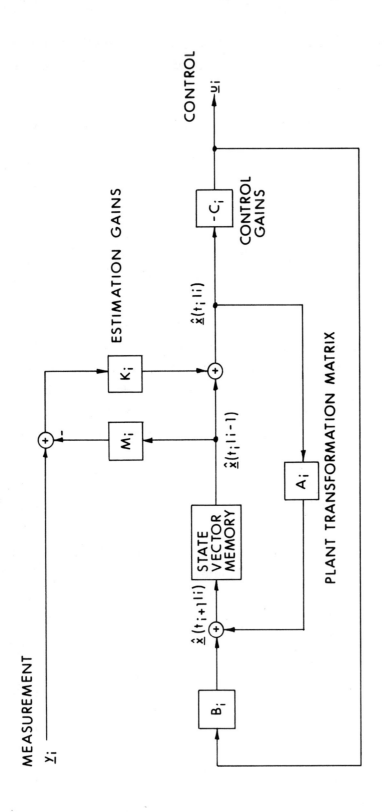

Fig. 3.1   The Structure of an Optimal Sampled-Data Controller

$$F_i = (A_i - B_i C_i)(I - K_i M_i) \qquad (3.37)$$

$$G_i = (A_i - B_i C_i) K_i \qquad (3.38)$$

In general, all elements of the matrices H, D, F, and G are non-trivial. At each sample instant $t_i$, the control computer must perform a number of multiplications equal to the number of elements in these matrices. A slightly smaller number of additions is also required.

If one does not need to maintain in the computer the explicit estimate $\underline{x}$ of the plant state, then the optimal controller is not unique. That is, the state space may be transformed in an infinite variety of ways while leaving unchanged the relationship of the input (measurement) sequence $\underline{y}_i$ and the output (control) sequence $\underline{u}_i$. This nonuniqueness can be exploited to minimize the required computer capacity, in terms of both the required gain storage and the required arithmetic. We will demonstrate two canonical forms for the state space representation, which both have $m^2$ less gains than the maximum (m is the dimension of the state space). This is a significant reduction, especially if it is high-dimensional state space.

The transformations producing the output-oriented or input-oriented canonical forms were developed earlier by Lee (1964) for the special case of single-input single-output constant gain systems. We have extended these canonical forms to the more general case of multi-input multi-output time-varying systems.

The state space may be transformed using any invertible transformation $S_i$:

$$\underline{v}_i = S_i \underline{x}_i \qquad (3.39)$$

In terms of the new state vector $\underline{v}$, the linear system of Eqs. (3.33) and (3.34) becomes

$$\underline{u}_i = R_i \underline{v}_i + D_i \underline{y}_i \qquad (3.40)$$

$$\underline{v}_{i+1} = Q_i \underline{v}_i + P_i \underline{y}_i \qquad (3.41)$$

49

where

$$Q_i = S_{i+1} F_i S_i^{-1} \qquad (3.42)$$

$$P_i = S_{i+1} G_i \qquad (3.43)$$

$$R_i = H_i S_i^{-1} \qquad (3.44)$$

Partition the matrix H into

$$H_i = \begin{bmatrix} \underline{h1}_i^T \\ \hline H'_i \end{bmatrix} \qquad (3.45)$$

Let the transformation S be given by

$$\underline{s1}_i^T = \underline{h1}_i^T$$

$$\underline{s2}_i^T = \underline{h1}_{i+1}^T F_i$$

$$\vdots$$

$$\underline{sm}_i^T = \underline{h1}_{i+m-1}^T F_{i+m-2} \cdots F_i$$

$$(3.46)$$

$$S_i = \begin{bmatrix} \underline{s1}_i^T \\ \vdots \\ \underline{sm}_i^T \end{bmatrix} \qquad (3.47)$$

50

Assume that the state is observable for all i through the first component u1 of the output vector. That is, if the input $\underline{y}$ is zero, the state $\underline{x}_i$ can be determined from the output sequence $u1_i \ldots u1_{i+m-1}$. This assumption is necessary to guarantee that $S^{-1}$ exists.

It can be shown that with the above transformation the linear system has been converted to the output-oriented canonical form

$$
\underline{u}_i = \begin{bmatrix} 1 & \underline{0}^T \\ \hline & R_i' \end{bmatrix} \underline{v}_i + D_i \underline{y}_i \tag{3.48}
$$

$$
\underline{v}_{i+1} = \begin{bmatrix} \underline{0} & I \\ \hline & q_i^T \end{bmatrix} \underline{v}_i + P_i \underline{y}_i \tag{3.49}
$$

where

$$
\underline{q}_i^T = \underline{sm}_{i+1}^T F_i S_i^{-1} \tag{3.50}
$$

$$
P_i = S_{i+1} G_i \tag{3.51}
$$

$$
R_i' = H_i' S_i^{-1} \tag{3.52}
$$

To prove that the new state transition matrix Q has the indicated form, note from Eq. (3.46) that the rows of the transformation S satisfy a recursion relation

$$
\underline{s(k+1)}_i^T = \underline{sk}_{i+1}^T F_i \tag{3.53}
$$

$$
k = 1, 2, \ldots m - 1
$$

51

One element of the state vector, according to Eq. (3.39), may be written

$$vk_{i+1} = \underline{sk}_{i+1}^T \; \underline{x}_{i+1} \tag{3.54}$$

which by Eq. (3.34) is

$$vk_{i+1} = \underline{sk}_{i+1}^T \; F_i \, \underline{x}_i + \underline{sk}_{i+1}^T \; G_i \, \underline{y}_i \tag{3.55}$$

and with Eq. (3.53) is

$$vk_{i+1} = \underline{s \; (k+1)}_i^T \; \underline{x}_i + \underline{sk}_{i+1}^T \; G_i \, \underline{y}_i \tag{3.56}$$

$$k = 1, \; 2 \; \ldots \; m - 1$$

and with Eq. (3.54) is

$$vk_{i+1} = v \; (k+1)_i + \underline{sk}_{i+1}^T \; G_i \, \underline{y}_i \tag{3.57}$$

$$k = 1, \; 2 \; \ldots \; m - 1$$

This proves Eq. (3.49).

To prove that the new state-to-output matrix R has the indicated form, note the first component of the output vector is according to Eqs. (3.33) and (3.45)

$$u1_i = \underline{h1}_i^T \; \underline{x}_i + D_i \, \underline{y}_i \tag{3.58}$$

By Eq. (3.46) this is the same as

$$u1_i = \underline{s1}_i^T \; \underline{x}_i + D_i \, \underline{y}_i \tag{3.59}$$

52

and with Eq. (3. 39) it is proved that

$$u1_i = v1_i + D_i \underline{y}_i \tag{3.60}$$

Figure 3. 2 illustrates the first canonical form for a system having only a single input and a single output. We call this the output-oriented canonical form, because with no further inputs $\underline{y}$ the elements of the state vector $\underline{v}$ at time $t_i$ are the next m outputs $u1_i \ldots u1_{i+m-1}$.

In computing the transformation matrix S, the arithmetic can be reduced if one uses a recursion formula for S. If one defines the matrices

$$D = \begin{bmatrix} \underline{0}^T & 0 \\ I & \underline{0} \end{bmatrix} \tag{3.61}$$

$$E_i = \begin{bmatrix} \underline{h1}_i^T \\ O \end{bmatrix} \tag{3.62}$$

then it is easily shown by considering definition (3. 46) that the set of matrices $S_i$ may be generated backward from

$$S_i = D S_{i+1} F_i + E_i \tag{3.63}$$

Or in words: $S_i$ can be formed from $S_{i+1}$ by postmultiplying $S_{i+1}$ by $F_i$, by moving all rows of the product down by one (throw away the bottom row), and by inserting $\underline{h1}_i^T$ as the new top row.

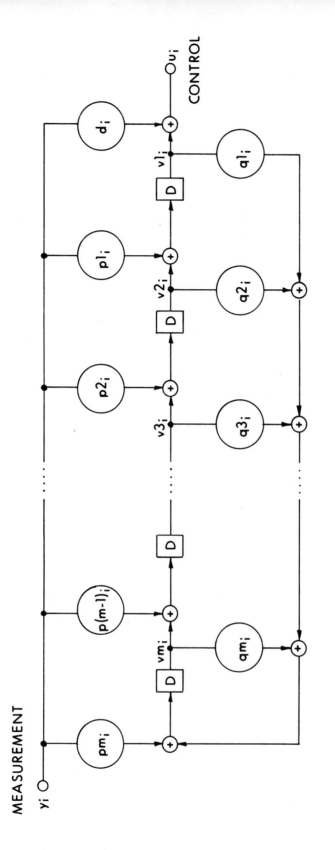

Fig. 3.2 A Canonical Form for Single-Input Single-Output Sampled-Data Controllers

54

An additional observation is that all the rows of $S_i$ are not defined by Eq. (3.46) near the terminal time. That is, $F_i$ and $\underline{h1}_i$ are given only for subscripts up to $i = L$. Thus with only $r$ intervals remaining to the terminal time, only the first $r$ rows of $S_i$ are defined. One may choose the bottom rows of $S_i$ by an arbitrary method. We have set the undefined rows to zero, and where the inverse of $S_i$ is required, we use the pseudoinverse. For recursion relation (3.63), the choice of initial condition which is equivalent is

$$S_{L+1} = 0 \qquad (3.64)$$

The second canonical form is the dual of the first canonical form. An analogous transformation is required:

$$\underline{x}_{i+1} = S_i \, \underline{v}_{i+1} \qquad (3.65)$$

Partition the matrix G into

$$G_i = \left[ \begin{array}{c|c} \underline{g1}_i & G_i' \end{array} \right] \qquad (3.66)$$

Let the columns of $S_i$ be given by

$$\underline{s1}_i = \underline{g1}_i$$

$$\underline{s2}_i = F_i \, \underline{g1}_{i-1} \qquad (3.67)$$

$$\vdots$$

$$\underline{sm}_i = F_i \, F_{i-1} \cdots F_{i-m+2} \, \underline{g1}_{i-m+1}$$

Assume that the state is controllable for all $i$ through the first component $y1$ of the input vector. That is, if all elements of the input vector $\underline{y}$ except $y1$ are zero and the state $\underline{x}_i$ is known, then the state $\underline{x}_{i+m}$ may be driven to zero

55

by applying the proper input sequence $y1_i \ldots y1_{i+m-1}$. This assumption is necessary to guarantee that $S^{-1}$ exists.

It can be shown that with the above transformation the linear system of Eqs. (3.33) and (3.34) has been converted to the input-oriented canonical form

$$\underline{u}_i = P_i \underline{v}_i + D_i \underline{y}_i \tag{3.68}$$

$$\underline{v}_{i+1} = \begin{bmatrix} \begin{bmatrix} \underline{0}^T \\ I \end{bmatrix} & \begin{vmatrix} \underline{q}_i \\ \cdot \end{vmatrix} \end{bmatrix} \underline{v}_i + \begin{bmatrix} \begin{bmatrix} 1 \\ \underline{0} \end{bmatrix} & R_i' \end{bmatrix} \underline{y}_i \tag{3.69}$$

where

$$\underline{q}_i = S_i^{-1} F_i \underline{sm}_{i-1} \tag{3.70}$$

$$P_i = H_i S_{i-1} \tag{3.71}$$

$$R_i' = S_i^{-1} G_i' \tag{3.72}$$

We omit the proof, as it is similar to the proof for the first canonical form. We call this the input-oriented canonical form, because if the state $\underline{v}_{i-m}$ was zero and all elements of the input vector $\underline{y}$ except $y1$ were zero, then the elements of the state vector $\underline{v}_i$ are the last m inputs $y1_{i-1} \ldots y1_{i-m}$.

There are other canonical forms having the minimum number of gains, but the two forms discussed here are perhaps the most useful. This is because they have the practical advantage that during intervals of operation when the system matrices H, D, F, and G are constant, these canonical forms are also constant. This situation arises in a stationary stochastic control problem during the operating period sufficiently after the initial time and sufficiently before the terminal time.

## 3.4 Synthesis of a Control Computer Program for an Air-to-Air Missile

To illustrate the cascade synthesis of Joseph and Tou as well as the transformation to a minimum arithmetic control computer program, let us consider the air-to-air missile guidance problem considered by Johansen (1964). The background of this problem is discussed in Appendix B. In the appendix we have stated the mathematical description of the problem. The fundamental differential equations governing the lateral displacement $y$ between the target and the missile normal to the initial line of sight, the lateral velocity $v$ between the target and the missile, and the random lateral acceleration $a_t$ of the target are given as

$$\frac{d}{dt}\begin{bmatrix} y \\ v \\ a_t \end{bmatrix} = \begin{bmatrix} 0 & 1 & 0 \\ 0 & 0 & 1 \\ 0 & 0 & -.4 \end{bmatrix}\begin{bmatrix} y \\ v \\ a_t \end{bmatrix} + \begin{bmatrix} 0 \\ -1 \\ 0 \end{bmatrix} a_m + \begin{bmatrix} 0 \\ 0 \\ n \end{bmatrix} \tag{3.73}$$

where the lateral missile acceleration $a_m$ is the control variable and the white noise $n$ produces the desired target activity. The covariance matrix $N$ of the white noise vector is given as

$$N = \begin{bmatrix} 0 & 0 & 0 \\ 0 & 0 & 0 \\ 0 & 0 & .2(32.2)^2/2.5 \end{bmatrix} \tag{3.74}$$

The covariance matrix $P$ of the initial plant state vector is

$$P = \begin{bmatrix} 0 & 0 & 0 \\ 0 & (200)^2 & 0 \\ 0 & 0 & (32.2)^2 \end{bmatrix} \tag{3.75}$$

The measurement of the line of sight angle $\sigma$ is given in terms of the plant state vector and the measurement noise $w$ as

$$\sigma = \begin{bmatrix} \dfrac{1}{3000\ t_{go}} & 0 & 0 \end{bmatrix} \begin{bmatrix} y \\ v \\ a_t \end{bmatrix} + w \tag{3.76}$$

The mean-square value of the measurement noise is nonstationary. At the i-th sample time its strength is

$$W_i = \frac{1}{\Delta t} \left[ \frac{15}{(3000\ t_{go_i})^2} + 1.5 \times 10^{-5} \right] \tag{3.77}$$

We wish to design a control computer program which will minimize the average value of the cost function

$$c = y(T)^2 + \int_0^T w_c\ a_m(t)^2\ dt \tag{3.78}$$

The cost includes the terminal miss-distance plus a weighted integral of the square of the missile lateral acceleration. Our strategy for finding the proper choice of the control weight $w_c$ is as follows: initially choose $w_c$ to be very small. Then design an optimal controller. Evaluate the design. In particular if at any time during the operating period the RMS missile acceleration exceeds 400 ft/sec.$^2$, then the design is not acceptable. Iteratively adjust the weighting $w_c$ until the peak RMS acceleration equals 400 ft/sec.$^2$

In the general notation, the cost weighting matrix Q for the terminal state is

$$Q = \begin{bmatrix} 1 & 0 & 0 \\ 0 & 0 & 0 \\ 0 & 0 & 0 \end{bmatrix} \tag{3.79}$$

During the operating period, the weighting matrix $W_{xx}$ for the plant state, the weighting matrix $W_{xu}$ for state and control, and the weighting matrix $W_{uu}$ for the control are given as

$$W_{xx} = \begin{bmatrix} 0 & 0 & 0 \\ 0 & 0 & 0 \\ 0 & 0 & 0 \end{bmatrix} \qquad W_{xu} = \begin{bmatrix} 0 \\ 0 \\ 0 \end{bmatrix} \qquad W_{uu} = \begin{bmatrix} w_c \end{bmatrix} \qquad (3.80)$$

In Appendix C we describe general-purpose subroutines for converting the continuous problem to sampled form (SAMPLSETUP), for computing the minimum variance linear estimator (ESTIMATOR), for computing the optimal control gains (CONTROLLER), for converting the state space representation of a control computer program into a minimum arithmetic standard form (STNDRDFORM), and for evaluating the average performance of the given control computer program (EVALUATOR). Using these general-purpose subroutines, it is a simple matter to write a main program which contains the mathematical problem statement and which calls the required subroutines to synthesize the optimal controller.

In our first attempt to produce an optimal design, we tried a penalty weight for the control of zero. That is, only terminal miss-distance was weighed in the cost. Unfortunately, the general-purpose design programs could not handle this case. In the controller design equations Eq. (3.5) the subroutine had a division overflow when trying to perform the indicated inversion. This numerical difficulty is related to the fact that the optimal sequence of control signals is not unique. For any initial state, a control exists for the last control interval which can drive the miss-distance to zero (in the noise-free measurable state control problem). Thus the control is completely arbitrary up to the last control interval. A proper choice of control is necessary in the last interval only, to assure that the cost is zero. Or expressed another way, in the noise-free measurable state control problem the quadratic form $x_{-i}^T \, Q_i \, x_{-i}$ is the minimum possible cost of the control process starting at time $t_i$ with state $x_i$. But the cost can be zero for any initial state starting at least one interval from the terminal time. Therefore all the $Q_i$ are theoretically zero matrices, after the first computation of Eq. (3.6). No control weight implies $U_i = 0$, and since in addition $Q_i = 0$ it is clear that in Eq. (3.5) we will attempt to invert zero. (Of course, the miss-distance will not be exactly zero in the stochastic problem. While

59

the same matrices $Q_i$ are appropriate to both the noise-free measurable state control problem and the stochastic control problem, it is not true that the quadratic form $\underline{x}_i^T Q_i \underline{x}_i$ represents the minimum possible cost in the stochastic problem).

We have chosen to bypass this numerical difficulty by introducing a very small weight on the control of $w_c = 10^{-9}$. This makes the optimization problem nontrivial, as there is now a trade-off between control effort and miss-distance. This procedure for avoiding the trouble was entirely satis-factory. The design proceeded automatically without further numerical difficulty.

In this illustration we asked for the optimal control computer program for a sample interval of $\Delta t = 0.8$ sec. and for an operating period of $T = 12$ sec. A flow chart of the operations required every cycle in the optimal con-trol computer program is given in Fig. 3.3. There are seven nontrivial coefficients used in the indicated multiplications. These coefficients in general are different for each computation cycle. The sequence of coeffi-cients required is shown in Table 3.1.

The performance of the missile under optimal control is shown in Fig. 3.4. The root-mean-square miss-distance is 31 ft. The peak RMS required missile acceleration is 250 ft/sec.$^2$ Since this is below the toler-ance level of 400 ft/sec.$^2$, it is not necessary to repeat the design procedure with a larger control weight. To verify that our choice of $w_c = 10^{-9}$ does not affect the design, we have repeated the design with the weight increased by an order-of-magnitude. The resulting performance of the optimal design was unchanged (miss-distance was the same to three figures).

60

Fig. 3.3    Flow Chart of the Operations Required Every Cycle in the
Missile Optimal Control Computer Program

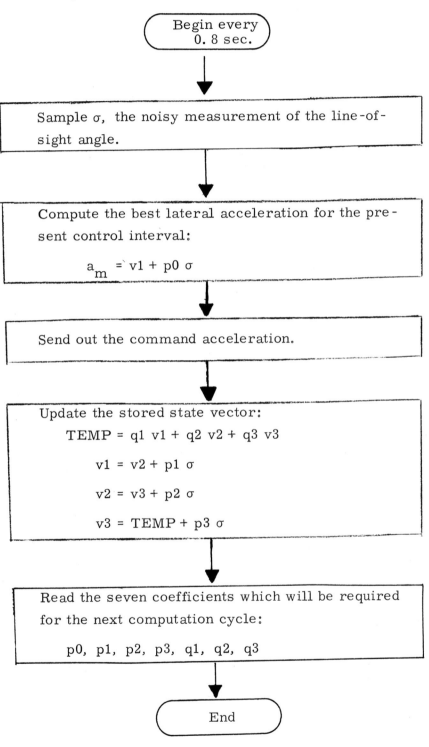

Table 3.1 The Sequence of Coefficients Used by the Missile Optimal Control Computer Program

| Sample Instant | Time To-Go | p0 | p1 | p2 | p3 | q1 | q2 | q3 |
|---|---|---|---|---|---|---|---|---|
| 1 | 12.0 | 0 | 0 | 0 | 0 | .175 | -.675 | 1.392 |
| 2 | 11.2 | 6497 | 703 | -706 | -914 | .137 | -.891 | 1.672 |
| 3 | 10.4 | 4753 | 392 | -1054 | -1327 | .244 | -1.226 | 1.906 |
| 4 | 9.6 | 3524 | 80 | -1366 | -1534 | .347 | -1.375 | 1.939 |
| 5 | 8.8 | 3287 | -172 | -1616 | -1554 | .361 | -1.302 | 1.835 |
| 6 | 8.0 | 3635 | -374 | -1793 | -1478 | .323 | -1.163 | 1.722 |
| 7 | 7.2 | 4188 | -618 | -1980 | -1392 | .287 | -1.056 | 1.640 |
| 8 | 6.4 | 4677 | -983 | -2225 | -1273 | .267 | -.972 | 1.563 |
| 9 | 5.6 | 5084 | -1529 | -2498 | -1020 | .252 | -.871 | 1.455 |
| 10 | 4.8 | 5541 | -2345 | -2696 | -498 | .232 | -.719 | 1.287 |
| 11 | 4.0 | 6170 | -3607 | -2564 | 403 | .203 | -.489 | 1.019 |
| 12 | 3.2 | 7041 | -5694 | -1302 | 1138 | .167 | -.109 | .510 |
| 13 | 2.4 | 8240 | -9542 | 4624 | 0 | 0 | 0 | 0 |
| 14 | 1.6 | 9996 | -18318 | 0 | 0 | 0 | 0 | 0 |
| 15 | 0.8 | 13019 | 0 | 0 | 0 | 0 | 0 | 0 |

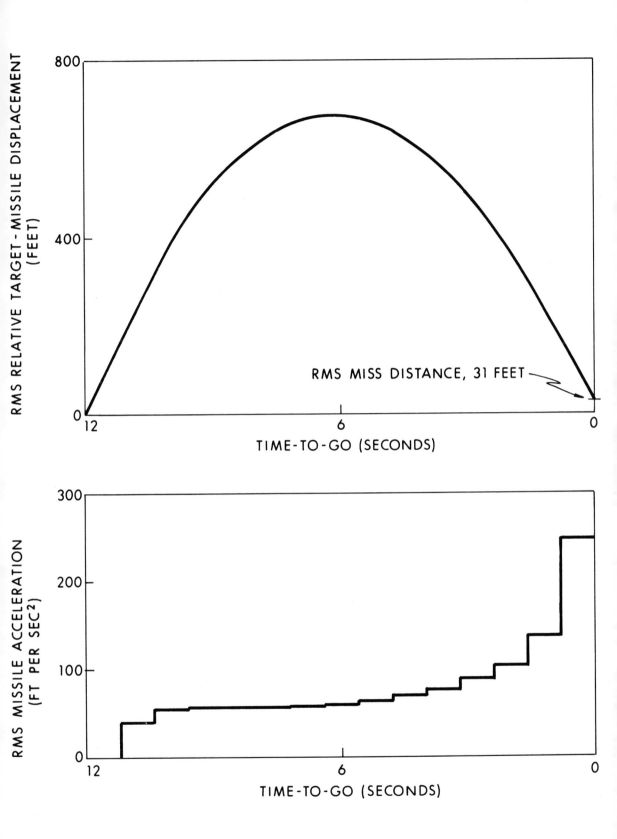

Fig. 3.4    Performance of the Missile under Optimal Control

Chapter 4

Applications of Optimal Controller Synthesis to the

Design of Computer-Limited Controllers

4.1 Introduction

In Chapter 3 we reviewed the techniques for synthesizing a linear sampled-data controller which will minimize the mean value of a quadratic cost function. If the data rate is fixed by the measurement devices and is not under computer control, then the resulting controller developed for the given data rate may be called an optimal controller. However, it is commonly the case that the instants at which the measurement devices are sampled are governed by the control computer program. Therefore we can explore various choices of sample rate in the search for the best design. In general increasing the sampling rate (shortening the sample period) permits tighter closed-loop control and improved performance. Therefore the optimal controller would be realized by synthesizing the control computer program for an infinitely small sample period.

But unfortunately the computational capacity of a control computer is limited. Even when reduced to a minimum arithmetic form, the control computer program designed according to measurement-limited optimal control theory will require an irreducible amount of computer time for each pass through the indicated operations. If the mathematical description of the plant includes n state variables, then as was shown in Chapter 3 the minimum arithmetic form will require 2n additions and 2n + 1 multiplications to realize an optimal measurement limited control program.

The best that one can do in attempting to use directly the measurement-limited synthesis theory is to first determine the time required by the given control computer to evaluate the indicated arithmetic operations in a nth-order minimum arithmetic form control computer program. Then

65

one can synthesize the optimal gain coefficients for a choice of sample interval which equals this required processing time. (If the computer must be time-shared among several activities, the choice of sample interval of course must be larger.)

One must realize, however, that while this procedure may design an efficient control computer program, it is not necessarily an optimal program. That is, in a computer-limited design problem, it is quite likely that a simpler control computer program would be superior to a program synthesized using optimal measurement-limited controller theory. The simpler program by operating at a faster repetition rate may provide tighter feedback control.

No general synthesis procedure exists for designing optimal computer-limited control computer programs. The best trade-off between feedback compensation complexity and the generally desirable shorter sample interval is approached largely by cut-and-try methods. However, optimal measurement-limited controller synthesis can be a valuable systematic aid in a computer-limited design problem. One of the obvious difficulties of any cut-and-try design method is that one does not know when he has reached the point of diminishing returns. One might terminate the design effort too soon, not realizing that a dramatic improvement in performance was possible using yet another design. Or more commonly one might continue to develop additional trial designs, looking for a dramatic improvement, when actually very little improvement in performance is possible. To avoid spending too little or too much time in the design effort, one can use optimal measurement-limited control theory to calculate bounds on the possible performance of computer-limited designs. Some examples are given in Section 4.2.

In these examples the theoretical optimal measurement-limited control computer program is synthesized only to gain knowledge of the possible performance. The details of the synthesized program are of no direct use, because the control computer lacks the capacity to implement the control program. Yet the algorithms for synthesizing optimal measurement-limited control programs are so straightforward that one looks for ways to use these algorithms for more than performance studies. One technique for using the synthesis algorithms to produce better computer-limited designs is to first simplify the problem dynamic description by substituting a lower-order approximate description for the more accurate problem description. The optimal control computer program for the approximate problem, since it is also of lower order, can be operated with a proportionately shorter sample interval. It is quite possible therefore that the optimal measurement-limited control computer program designed with respect to the simplified problem description can outperform the higher-order control program which required the longer sample interval. As an illustration of this technique, in Section 4.3 we will consider the air-to-air missile control problem. We will show that the controller synthesized with respect to an approximate (second-order) process description indeed outperforms the controller synthesized with respect to the more exact (third-order) process description.

In addition to arithmetic speed other aspects of the control computer may affect the design. Memory storage capacity is another common limitation. The theoretical optimal control computer programs can require a large amount of fixed storage capacity, because in general the gain coefficients are different for each computation cycle. The amount of storage required to hold the sequence of minimum arithmetic coefficients is directly proportional to the number of computation cycles in the anticipated operating period. If the required storage exceeds the available capacity, then the designer must simplify his design at the expense of the resulting performance. One possible method for reducing the storage required is to fit polynomials or other functions to the optimal sequence of coefficients. The control computer program would calculate the current gains in real time by evaluating the functions. Of course, one must examine the performance of such an approximate realization of the optimal controller. The resulting performance may have been degraded beyond acceptable limits.

A special case of polynomial fits to the sequences of optimal gains is given by constant gain controllers. If a constant gain controller can provide acceptable performance, it has many practical advantages: The necessity of storing gain sequences is eliminated. No computer time must be spent computing the gains from functions. Furthermore the control computer program does not have to keep track of the time-elapsed from the initial time or the time-to-go to the terminal time, because the

gains are independent of time. In Sec. 4.4 we design a constant coefficient control computer program for the Apollo attitude control autopilot
using the algorithms for optimal time-varying controller synthesis.

## 4.2 Computation of Bounds on the Possible Performance of Computer-Limited Designs

In Sec. 2.6 we evaluated the short burn performance of a spacecraft steering law. The results were illustrated in Fig. 2.5. The peak
nozzle excursion angle was 2.7 degrees RMS. The cut-off velocity error
was 7.1 ft/sec. One might conclude that since the peak RMS nozzle angle
is close to the hard limit of 5 degrees, there is no margin for improving
the operation with an alternate linear controller. An alternate steering
computer program could not do much better at reducing the cut-off error.
Should efforts at refining the steering program cease at this point?

An answer to this question can be found by evaluating the performance of an optimal steering computer program. (We will not repeat
here the mathematical description of the problem given in Appendix A
and expanded in Sec. 2.6). Using the algorithms for synthesizing optimal control computer programs we design the program which will minimize the average value of the cost:

$$\text{cost} = \left[ \frac{1}{2} M v_1^2 + \frac{1}{2} I \omega^2 \right]_{t=T} + \int_0^T w (\delta - \epsilon)^2 dt \qquad (4.1)$$

The term in the brackets is the kinetic energy of the vehicle at cut-off
due to lateral velocity error $v_1$ and due to the tumbling rate $\omega$. The integral penalizes the excursions of the main engine nozzle angle $\delta$ away
from the angular location $\epsilon$ of the center-of-mass. For an operating
period of T = 20 sec., for a sample interval of $\Delta t$ = 2 sec., and for a
choice of nozzle weight of w = $10^6$, the performance of the optimal closed-
loop steering program is shown in Fig. 4.1. The value of the minimum
average cost is 2600 ft.-lb., compared with an average cost of 55,000
ft.-lb. for the constant-gain cross-product steer law. Under optimal control the cut-off velocity error is only .08 ft. per sec. RMS; the cut-off
rotation rate is .06 deg. per sec. RMS. The peak nozzle angle is 2.7
degrees RMS. Comparing this with the cross-product steer-law performance, which was shown in Fig. 2.5, we see that the terminal energy

68

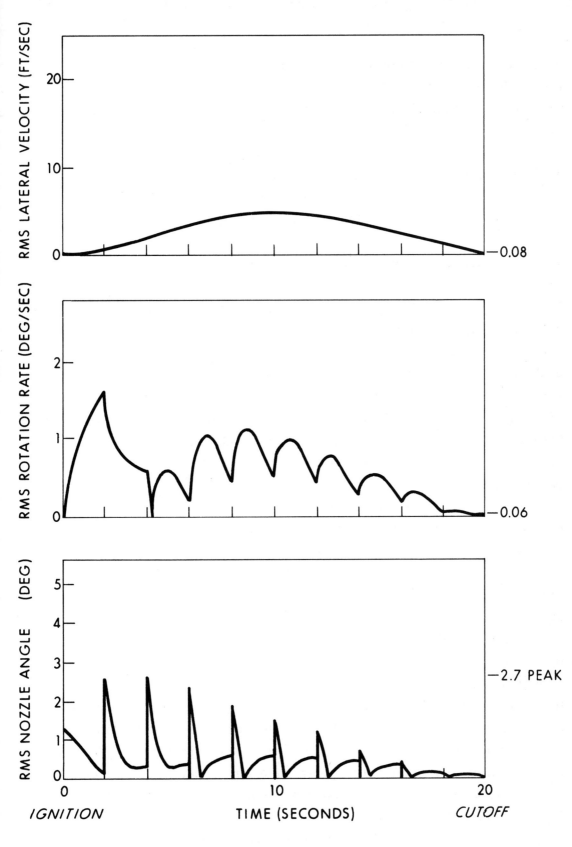

Fig. 4.1    Performance of the Optimal Steer Law

can be reduced to negligible levels with no increase in peak nozzle activity. Thus the answer to our original question is: yes, continued effort should be applied toward refining the practical steering computer
program.

In Sec. 3.4 we synthesized the control computer program for an
air-to-air missile which minimized the average value of the cost:

$$\text{cost} = y(T)^2 + \int_0^T w \, a_m(t)^2 \, dt \qquad (4.2)$$

The first term is the square of the terminal miss-distance. The integral penalizes the missile acceleration $a_m$ used to intercept the target.
For an operating period of T = 12 sec., for a sample interval of $\Delta t$ = .8
sec., and for a choice of control weight w = $10^{-9}$ (negligibly small) the
optimally controlled process had a miss distance of 31 ft. RMS with a
peak missile acceleration of 250 ft. per sec.$^2$. (Recall Fig. 3.4.) Now
suppose the choice of sample interval $\Delta t$ = .8 sec. was dictated because
of the time required for the on-board computer to evaluate each cycle of
the third-order control computer program. The question then arises,
could a lower-order controller perform better by permitting a shorter
sample period $\Delta t$?

One can obtain a partial answer to this question by evaluating the
performance of the optimal controller for each of several choices of
sample interval $\Delta t$. We have done this for sample intervals of 1.0, .8,
.6, .4, .2, and .1. The mathematical description of dynamic process
is as is given in Appendix B. The synthesis and evaluation of the optimal control program for each choice of sample interval proceeds as in
the design example in Sec. 3.4. We find that for the larger sample intervals (1.0, .8, and .6), the negligibly small control weight of w = $10^{-9}$
may be used; the resulting peak RMS missile acceleration is below the
tolerable limit of 400 ft. per sec.$^2$. On the other hand, for the smaller
sample intervals (.4, .2, and .1), with the negligibly small control weight
the optimal controller will call for a missile acceleration exceeding the
tolerable limit. Therefore one must use a larger penalty on the controlling acceleration to produce an optimal design whose peak acceleration
is just at the limit of 400 ft. per sec.$^2$.

There is no explicit formula for selecting the exact choice of weighting to produce the desired result. One must use an iterative technique to

find the proper choice. The entire synthesis procedure, from selecting a weight w to evaluating the peak acceleration f under optimal control, defines a nonlinear function f(w). We wish to find the value of w such that the resulting f is equal to the desired value $f_d$ = 400. We have used the linear interpolation method (see Householder (1953) or Hildebrand (1956) or Hamming (1962) ) to converge iteratively to the desired solution. Given $f(w_2)$ the peak acceleration for the next-to-last choice of weight and given $f(w_1)$ the peak acceleration for the last choice of weight, the next estimate of the solution value $w_0$ is computed as

$$w_0 = \frac{f(w_1) - f_d}{f(w_1) - f(w_2)} w_2 + \frac{f_d - f(w_2)}{f(w_1) - f(w_2)} w_1 \qquad (4.3)$$

The new choice of weight will yield a design hopefully with the peak acceleration closer to the desired level $f_d$. The iterative step is illustrated in Fig. 4.2. To guarantee that the method will converge, one should accept the trial weight $w_0$ only if it produces a peak acceleration which is closer to the desired acceleration than was the value previously found using $w_1$. Should the trail weight fail this test, select another trail weight which is closer to the previous weight $w_1$. We chose to program a retreat to the geometric mean of $w_1$ and $w_0$

$$w_0' = \sqrt{w_1 w_0} \qquad (4.4)$$

Eventually a new value for $w_0$ produces a design which is closer to the desired level. Now one proceeds to the next stage of the iteration. Relabeling $w_1$ as $w_2$ and $w_0$ as $w_1$, etc., we return to the linear interpolation formula Eq. (4.3) to select a new trail weight. This procedure continues until the result is within a preselected tolerance of the desired level. One other protection should be incorporated into the iterative steps: do not use an extrapolation proposed by Eq. (4.3) if it is a negative weight. We chose to prevent this by requiring that $w_0$ be no smaller than .01 $w_1$.

In Fig. 4.3 we have plotted the results of this study. The miss-distance of the air-to-air missile under optimal control is shown for various choices of the sample interval $\Delta t$. For the large sample intervals ($\Delta t$ = .6 and larger) the peak RMS acceleration $a_p$ was below the tolerable

71

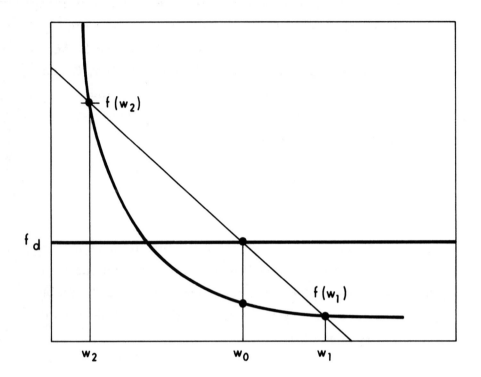

Fig. 4.2  Linear Interpolation Used to Converge to the Solution
of $f(w) = f_d$

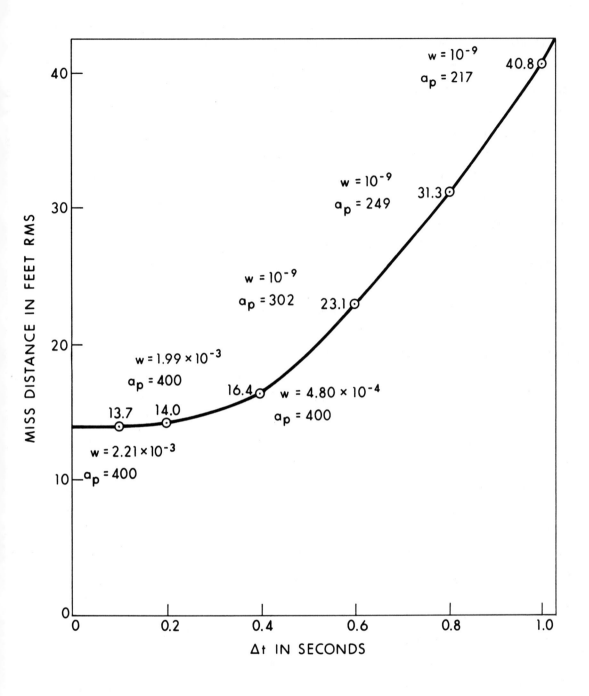

Fig. 4.3   The Miss-Distance of the Air-to-Air Missile Under Optimal
Control for Various Choices of the Sample Interval

limit without having to use a nonnegligible control weight w. For the small sample intervals ($\Delta t$ = . 4 and smaller) an appropriate weight w had to be found to constrain the peak acceleration to 400 ft. /sec.$^2$. The results clearly show that reducing the sample period permits the optimal controller to perform better. A point of diminishing returns is reached at about $\Delta t$ = . 2 sec. Reducing the sample interval further by one-half to $\Delta t$ = . 1 sec. permits little improvement in performance. We can infer by extrapolation that the optimal continuous controller would probably have a miss-distance of between 13 and 14 feet RMS.

We assumed that . 8 sec. would be required to process a third-order control computer program. Using the optimal controller for $\Delta t$ = . 8 (which is third-order) the miss-distance would be 31 ft. RMS. Yet in the absence of computer limitations there exist controllers with miss-distances as small as 14 ft. RMS. Thus the answer to our question is: it is quite possible that there are control computer programs of lower order than the third-order optimal measurement-limited program for $\Delta t$ = . 8 sec., which perform better by permitting a shorter sample period.

In Appendix A we discussed the Apollo spacecraft control problem. Here one must design a control computer program to process the measurements of attitude and velocity and produce commands to the gimballed main engine. Considering the pitch plane only, this requires a controller having two inputs and one output. Because of the many responsibilities assigned to the on-board guidance computer, one wishes to perform the control function reasonably well but with as little use of the computer capacity as is possible. We can use optimal measurement-limited control theory to help choose appropriate sampling rates for the attitude measurements and the velocity measurements. We can calculate the optimal performance if nearly continuous sampling is employed. Then we can explore the increase in the minimum cost as a function of lengthing the sample period used for either attitude or velocity.

As is discussed in Appendix A, the fundamental equation governing the vehicle is

$$
\begin{bmatrix} \dot{\epsilon} \\ \dot{v}_\perp \\ \dot{\omega} \\ \dot{\theta} \\ \dot{v}_b \\ \dot{q} \\ \dot{\delta} \end{bmatrix}
=
\begin{bmatrix}
0 & 0 & 0 & 0 & 0 & 0 & 0 \\
0 & 0 & 0 & 10 & 0 & -1.3 & -10 \\
-1.13 & 0 & 0 & 0 & 0 & .081 & 1.13 \\
0 & 0 & 1 & 0 & 0 & 0 & 0 \\
11 & 0 & 0 & 0 & 0 & -100 & -11 \\
0 & 0 & 0 & 0 & 1 & 0 & 0 \\
0 & 0 & 0 & 0 & 0 & 0 & -10
\end{bmatrix}
\begin{bmatrix} \epsilon \\ v_\perp \\ \omega \\ \theta \\ v_b \\ q \\ \delta \end{bmatrix}
+
\begin{bmatrix} 0 \\ 0 \\ 0 \\ 0 \\ 0 \\ 0 \\ 10 \end{bmatrix} \delta_c
+
\begin{bmatrix} 0 \\ -10 \\ 1.13 \\ 0 \\ -11 \\ 0 \\ 0 \end{bmatrix} n \quad (4.5)
$$

The measurement vector available to the computer is

$$
\begin{bmatrix} v_a \\ \theta_a \end{bmatrix}
=
\begin{bmatrix}
0 & 1 & 0 & 0 & -1.3 & 0 & 0 \\
0 & 0 & 0 & 1 & 0 & -.13 & 0
\end{bmatrix}
\begin{bmatrix} \epsilon \\ v_\perp \\ \omega \\ \theta \\ v_b \\ q \\ \delta \end{bmatrix}
+
\begin{bmatrix} w_v \\ w_\theta \end{bmatrix}
\quad (4.6)
$$

The seventh-order vehicle-state vector includes: the angular offset $\epsilon$ of the center-of-mass of the unbent vehicle (the angle away from the centerline as seen from the engine gimbal station), the unwanted component $v_\perp$ of the velocity of the center-of-mass of the vehicle (perpendicular to the initial velocity-to-be-gained), the angular velocity $\omega$ of the underlying rigid vehicle, the inertial attitude $\theta$ of the underlying rigid vehicle relative to the reference direction (the initial direction of the velocity-to-be-gained), the velocity $v_b$ of the generalized bending coordinate, the displacement $q$ of the generalized bending coordinate, and the angle $\delta$ of the nozzle of the main engine relative to the centerline of the end of the vehicle. The control variable is the nozzle angle commanded $\delta_c$. The white noise n(t) disturbs the state of the vehicle as a random component of the thrust vector perpendicular to the centerline of the end of the vehicle. The two components of the measurement vector are: the velocity $v_a$ of the vehicle at the measurement-unit station due to translation and bending (resolved perpendicular to the reference direction) and the attitude at the measurement-unit station due to rigid rotation plus bending (relative to the reference direction). Corrupting the measurements are noises $w_v$ and $w_\theta$.

The covariance matrix N of the white noise vector disturbing the state is given by the outer product

$$N = .0004 \begin{bmatrix} 0 \\ -10 \\ 1.13 \\ 0 \\ -11 \\ 0 \\ 0 \end{bmatrix} \begin{bmatrix} 0 & -10 & 1.13 & 0 & -11 & 0 & 0 \end{bmatrix} \qquad (4.7)$$

The mean value of the initial state vector is zero. The covariance matrix of the initial state vector is

$$P = \begin{bmatrix} (.02)^2 & 0 & 0 & 0 & 0 & 0 & 0 \\ 0 & 0 & 0 & 0 & 0 & 0 & 0 \\ 0 & 0 & 0 & 0 & 0 & 0 & 0 \\ 0 & 0 & 0 & (.01)^2 & 0 & 0 & 0 \\ 0 & 0 & 0 & 0 & 0 & 0 & 0 \\ 0 & 0 & 0 & 0 & 0 & 0 & 0 \\ 0 & 0 & 0 & 0 & 0 & 0 & 0 \end{bmatrix} \qquad (4.8)$$

That is, the center-of-mass offset has a RMS value of .02 radians, and the initial attitude error has an RMS value of .01 radians.

The covariance matrix W of the measurement noise vector is assumed to be

$$W = \begin{bmatrix} (.2)^2/12 & 0 \\ 0 & (.0002)^2/12 \end{bmatrix} \qquad (4.9)$$

As discussed in the Appendix, this choice is related to the quantization size of the analogue-to-digital conversion of the measurements: .2 ft/sec.

76

for the integrating accelerometers and .0002 radians for the measure-ment-unit attitude read-out.

Because of the unknown offset angle of the center-of-mass, the ini-tial thrust vector direction cannot be aligned perfectly. There is an ini-tial torque due to this thrust misalignment; this causes the vehicle to turn away from its initial direction. The white noise lateral vibration compo-nent of the thrust vector also disturbs the state of the vehicle, especially the bending mode. Therefore feedback control is required to steer the vehicle to the terminal conditions and perhaps to stabilize the bending mode. We summarize the objective of the control action in terms of a cost function:

$$\text{cost} = \left[ \frac{1}{2} M v_\perp^2 + \frac{1}{2} I \omega^2 \right]_{t = T} + \int_0^T w \dot{\delta}^2 \, dt \qquad (4.10)$$

The terms in the brackets are the kinetic energy at cut-off due to the un-wanted component of velocity $v_\perp$ and due to the vehicle rotation rate. The prinicpal objective of performing the short burn is to null the velocity-to-be-gained vector including the component $v_\perp$. (In this linear problem we do not discuss the possibility of a parallel component in the cut-off velo-city error vector. It is assumed that this component is nulled satisfac-torily by timing precisely the instant of the shut-down of thrust.) A sec-ondary requirement is that the rotation rate $\omega$ of the vehicle should be small at cut-off. Otherwise attitude control jets will have to be fired to arrest the tumbling after shut-down. This would waste precious attitude control fuel. It turns out that combining the cost due to velocity and ro-tation rate as kinetic energies yields quite reasonable performance in the resulting optimal design. Were this not so, a different relative em-phasis upon minimizing velocity or rotation rate would have to be adopted.

We have not included initially any penalty on bending energy. If during the short burn the energy in the bending mode under optimal con-trol exceeds tolerable levels, then we must add to the cost a penalty on bending energy to constrain the resulting design. It turns out that this is not required.

The nozzle actuator in linear operation produces a nozzle angular rate $\dot{\delta}$ proportional to the difference between the commanded angle $\delta_c$ and the actual nozzle angle $\delta$ (see Eq. (4.5)). But the drive system of

77

the actuator has a maximum rate capability of .1 radian per second. Therefore to assure that the resulting design will operate as designed by the linear theory, we have included in the cost a penalty of the nozzle rate. We will chose the weight w placed upon the integral of the square of nozzle rate so that the resulting optimal design has a peak nozzle angular rate of .05 radians per sec. RMS. In addition the actual nozzle will hit a position limit at an angle of .1 radian. If penalizing the nozzle rate does not also satisfactorily limit the nozzle position, we can later add a penalty on position.

In the general matrix notation, the terminal cost weighting matrix Q for this problem is

$$
Q = \begin{bmatrix}
0 & 0 & 0 & 0 & 0 & 0 & 0 \\
0 & 1100 & 0 & 0 & 0 & 0 & 0 \\
0 & 0 & 185000 & 0 & 0 & 0 & 0 \\
0 & 0 & 0 & 0 & 0 & 0 & 0 \\
0 & 0 & 0 & 0 & 0 & 0 & 0 \\
0 & 0 & 0 & 0 & 0 & 0 & 0 \\
0 & 0 & 0 & 0 & 0 & 0 & 0
\end{bmatrix}
\tag{4.11}
$$

The cost weighting matrices for the vehicle state $\underline{x}$ and the control variable u (i. e. $\delta_c$), which appear in the integral quadratic cost, are

$$
W_{xx} = \begin{bmatrix}
0 & 0 & 0 & 0 & 0 & 0 & 0 \\
0 & 0 & 0 & 0 & 0 & 0 & 0 \\
0 & 0 & 0 & 0 & 0 & 0 & 0 \\
0 & 0 & 0 & 0 & 0 & 0 & 0 \\
0 & 0 & 0 & 0 & 0 & 0 & 0 \\
0 & 0 & 0 & 0 & 0 & 0 & 0 \\
0 & 0 & 0 & 0 & 0 & 0 & 100w
\end{bmatrix}
\qquad
W_{xu} = \begin{bmatrix}
0 \\ 0 \\ 0 \\ 0 \\ 0 \\ 0 \\ -100w
\end{bmatrix}
\qquad
W_{uu} = [100\,w]
\tag{4.12}
$$

We considered various basic sample intervals for sending out nozzle angle commands. These included .05, .1, .25, and 1 sec. intervals. It was assumed that the velocity measurements and attitude measurements would be taken at fixed integer multiples of the basic control sample interval. For example, if the basic sample interval was .1 sec., the attitude might be sampled every interval and the velocity might be sampled every tenth interval. In this case the measurement sample intervals would be $\Delta t_\theta = .1$ and $\Delta t_v = 1$. The estimator of the state each .1 sec. would incorporate an attitude measurement. In addition periodically every 1 sec. it must also incorporate a velocity measurement.

In this situation the measurement vector at some instants is one-dimensional and at the other instants is two-dimensional. In the numerical study of the performance of the optimal controller, rather than vary the measurement dimension periodically, it is convenient to assume that the measurement vector is always two-dimensional. The unwanted component is then effectively shut off by periodically varying the variance of the measurement noise. When both measurements are to be incorporated, the covariance of the measurement noise is assumed to be as given by Eq. (4.9). But when one component is not to be used, we will set the variance of the noise for that component to a very large number $(10^{10})$. The optimal filter will therefore apply very small estimator gains to the measurement component, and the net effect on the state estimate will be negligible.

It is a straightforward matter to write a main computer program which contains the mathematical description of the control problem. The choice of sample rate mix is read into the program from a data card, and the periodic measurement noise is constructed accordingly. The program contains a main loop which calls for optimal designs for assumed values of weighting on the square of the nozzle rate. This loop is repeated using the linear interpolation method to find the proper choice of weight to produce the desired nozzle activity. Each pass through this loop requires the use of several subprograms to perform the routine tasks: SAMPLSETUP to convert the continuous problem to sampled form, ESTIMATOR to design the minimum variance state estimator, CONTROLLER to design the noise-free measurable-state optimal controller, SENSLIMDES to form the state space representation of the sensor-limited optimal stochastic controller (the cascade of the estimator and controller), and EVALUATOR to determine the RMS values of the quantities of interest and the mean cost when the vehicle is operated by this controller.

The results of the study are summarized in Table 4.1. Here we display the achievable mean terminal error energy E of the vehicle due to velocity error and vehicle rotation rate for the assumed sample interval mix. Also tabulated are the values of weight w which were required to hold the peak RMS nozzle rate to .05 radians per sec. It is interesting to note that the unwanted energy rises steeply as the choice of attitude sample interval $\Delta t_\theta$ is increased. On the other hand, we can increase the velocity sample interval $\Delta t_v$, and the energy rises only gradually. This must be a result of the relative size of the measurement quantizations (.2 ft/sec. for velocity and .0002 radians for attitude). Apparently an optimal estimator can determine adequately the unwanted velocity $v_\perp$ by using the accurate attitude measurements together with the known vehicle dynamics. The direct measurement of the velocity adds little information because it is so noisy. We conclude that a practical system of subprograms in the guidance computer of this vehicle may be organized with a short sample interval control loop measuring only vehicle attitude and a longer sample interval control loop measuring only vehicle velocity. The separation of guidance steering and attitude control as described in Appendix A may be considered an example of this type of system.

The unwanted energy rises steeply if the basic control sample interval is made larger than .1 sec. This is probably strongly related to the nozzle actuator time constant of .1 sec. For sample intervals shorter than one time constant, we can keep the nozzle going near the maximum desired rate. But for sample intervals longer than one time constant, the nozzle may be utilized at near maximum rate right after the new nozzle angle command is received, but the rate quickly decays to zero as the nozzle angle reaches the commanded angle. The average effective nozzle speed available is inversely proportional to the length of the sample period.

A practical choice of sample interval mix would appear to be a basic sample interval of .1 sec. for the attitude measurements (and the nozzle commands) combined with a sample interval of 1.0 sec. for the velocity measurements. This sampling mix will permit lower usage of the computer capacity without ruling out performance close to the theoretical optimum possible under shorter sample interval control.

Table 4.1      Achievable Mean Terminal Error Energy of the Apollo Spacecraft for Various Sampling Intervals

| $\Delta t_\theta$ \ $\Delta t_v$ | .05 | .1 | .25 | 1 | ∞ |
|---|---|---|---|---|---|
| .05 | E = 299<br>w=8.21×10$^4$<br>$\Delta t$ = .05 | | | | |
| .1 | | E = 633<br>w=2.39×10$^5$<br>$\Delta t$ = .1 | | E = 678<br>w=2.59×10$^5$<br>$\Delta t$ = .1 | |
| .25 | | | E=8.86×10$^3$<br>w=8.76×10$^6$<br>$\Delta t$ = .25 | E=1.94×10$^4$<br>w=3.10×10$^7$<br>$\Delta t$ = .25 | E=1.42×10$^4$<br>w=7.10×10$^6$<br>$\Delta t$ = .25 |
| 1 | | | E=1.19×10$^5$<br>w=3.38×10$^8$<br>$\Delta t$ = .25 | E=9.86×10$^5$<br>w=1.18×10$^9$<br>$\Delta t$ = 1 | E=1.01×10$^6$<br>w=1.11×10$^9$<br>$\Delta t$ = 1 |
| ∞ | | | | E=1.30×10$^6$<br>w=7.08×10$^8$<br>$\Delta t$ = 1 | E=1.81×10$^6$ |

E     Error energy.

w     The weight required to hold the peak nozzle rate to .05 radian/sec. RMS.

$\Delta t$     The basic sample interval at which the nozzle is commanded.

$\Delta t_v$     Velocity measurement sample interval.

$\Delta t_\theta$     Attitude measurement sample interval.

An interesting anomaly is shown in Table 4.1 for the choice of measurement sample interval of .25 sec. One sees a lower achievable terminal energy for the case where velocity information is never used ($\Delta t_y = \infty$) than in a case where velocity information is used ($\Delta t_v = 1.0$). Clearly this contradicts the notion of optimality. If a controller processes the measurements in an optimal fashion, then adding more sources of information cannot degrade the possible performance. This anomaly is due to the method we used to constrain the peak RMS value of nozzle rate. We used a flat weighted integral of the square of nozzle rate in the cost as a convenient way of constraining the peak rate. The resulting designs therefore are not truly optimal, because one can conceive of a time-varying weight which will yield a design having nozzle rate at the maximum over a broader period of time. With the stronger control, lower terminal energies can be achieved. Figure 4.4 shows the RMS values of the nozzle rate in the two designs. The design which had the lower terminal energy indeed happened to have a broad period of peak nozzle rate.

## 4.3 The Design of Lower-Order Time-Varying Controllers; Optimal Designs for Approximate Problems

A theoretical result of optimal stochastic control theory is that in general the order of the optimal controller must equal the order of the process being controlled. This immediately raises a practical difficulty in applying optimal controller synthesis to actual problems. Most actual dynamic processes are extremely complex. A spacecraft, for example, has a whole family of natural bending modes and fuel slosh modes. If the designer uses an exhaustive mathematical description of the process as a starting point in the controller synthesis, the resulting optimal design will be of such high order that its implementation will be impractical.

Obviously the designer must first make reasonable simplifications in the problem description. High-frequency modes with sufficient natural damping can be discarded as not requiring active attention from the controller. Other modes in the plant, only weakly controllable or observable, might be discarded in optimizing another portion of the control system. Eventually the designer reaches a point where he is not confident that further simplifications in the mathematical model for the plant are possible.

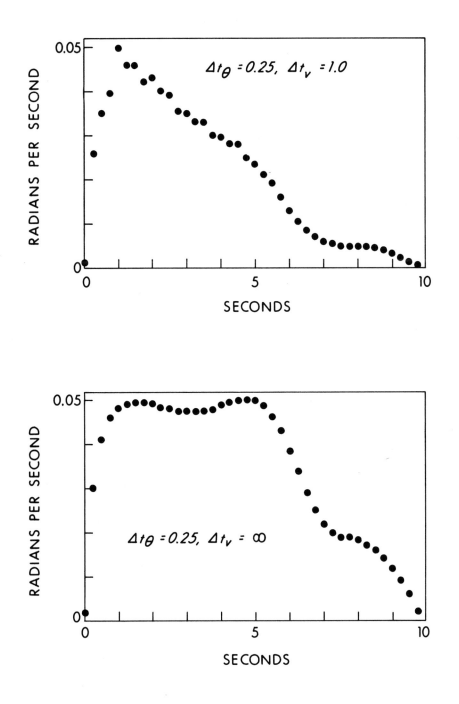

Fig. 4.4　The RMS Nozzle Angular Velocity of the Apollo
　　　　　Spacecraft Under Optimal Control for Two Choices
　　　　　of Sample Interval Mix

Yet in a computer-limited application, if one cannot start with a very simplified model, then the resulting controller synthesized by optimal control theory will require too much computer time.

At this point a possible technique for developing less complex time-varying controllers is: Go ahead and make some additional simplifications in the mathematical model. Design the related lower-order optimal controller. But evaluate the performance of the simplified controller with respect to the more complex description of the plant. In this way one may succeed in designing a simplified controller having reasonable performance — in fact, possibly better performance than the higher-order optimal controller designed and implemented at a slower sampling rate.

As an example of this technique we consider again the air-to-air missile control problem. Johansen (1964) suggested a way to simplify the third-order description of the problem. The state variables in the problem had been the relative lateral distance y between the target and the missile (measured normal to the initial line-of-sight), the relative lateral velocity v between the target and the missile, and the correlated lateral acceleration $a_t$ of the target alone. Johansen suggested that perhaps the evasive acceleration $a_t$ of the target could be replaced by a white noise having the same low-frequency power density, thus eliminating one state variable. We can try this suggestion in our sampled-data problem,

$$\frac{d}{dt} \begin{bmatrix} y \\ v \end{bmatrix} = \begin{bmatrix} 0 & 1 \\ 0 & 0 \end{bmatrix} \begin{bmatrix} y \\ v \end{bmatrix} + \begin{bmatrix} 0 \\ -1 \end{bmatrix} a_m + \begin{bmatrix} 0 \\ a_t \end{bmatrix} \tag{4.13}$$

where the missile lateral acceleration $a_m$ is still the control variable and $a_t$ is now a white noise. In the third-order model, $a_t$ had an RMS value of 32.2 ft/sec$^2$. and a correlation time of 2.5 sec. To match low-frequency power densities of the third- and second-order descriptions, this requires that the autocorrelation of the white noise $a_t$ be given as

$$E \, a_t(t_1) \, a_t(t_2) = 2(32.2)^2 \, 2.5 \ \delta(t_1 - t_2) \tag{4.14}$$

where $\delta$ is the Dirac delta function. The covariance matrix N of the white noise disturbance vector is therefore

84

$$N = \begin{bmatrix} 0 & 0 \\ 0 & 2(32.2)^2 2.5 \end{bmatrix} \qquad (4.15)$$

The measurement of the line-of-sight angle $\sigma$ is described by

$$\sigma = \begin{bmatrix} \dfrac{1}{3000\, t_{go}} & 0 \end{bmatrix} \begin{bmatrix} y \\ v \end{bmatrix} + w \qquad (4.16)$$

As in the third order problem, the covariance W of the measurement noise w is given as

$$W_i = \frac{1}{\Delta t} \left[ \frac{15}{(3000\, t_{go_i})^2} + 1.5 \times 10^{-5} \right] \qquad (4.17)$$

The covariance matrix P of the initial plant state vector is

$$P = \begin{bmatrix} 0 & 0 \\ 0 & (200)^2 \end{bmatrix} \qquad (4.18)$$

As before, the design objective is to find the controller which will minimize the average squared miss-distance while using controlling missile acceleration having peak RMS acceleration less than 400 ft./sec.$^2$. So we use the same cost function:

$$\text{cost} = y(T)^2 + \int_0^T w_c\, a_m(t)^2\, dt \qquad (4.19)$$

In terms of the two-dimensional state space representation for the process, this calls for a cost weighting matrix Q for the terminal state of

$$Q = \begin{bmatrix} 1 & 0 \\ 0 & 0 \end{bmatrix} \qquad (4.20)$$

During the operating period, the weighting matrix $W_{xx}$ for the plant state, the weighting matrix $W_{xu}$ for state and control, and the weighting matrix $W_{uu}$ for the control must be

$$W_{xx} = \begin{bmatrix} 0 & 0 \\ 0 & 0 \end{bmatrix} \qquad W_{xu} = \begin{bmatrix} 0 \\ 0 \end{bmatrix} \qquad W_{uu} = [w_c] \qquad (4.21)$$

We shall assume a simple linear relationship for the required controller computation time as a function of the order of the control computer program: A zero-order controller (pure gain) will require .2 sec., first-order .4 sec., second-order .6 sec., and third-order .8 sec. Recall that the number of multiplications required in a nth-order canonical form control computer program is $2n + 1$. Thus we are assuming that .1 sec is required for each multiply, and an additional .1 sec. is required for fixed overhead.

The second-order $\Delta t = .6$ sec. controller is designed by the general-purpose synthesis subroutines (Appendix C). This design is the optimal control computer program for the simplified second-order problem. We used again an operating period of $T = 12$ sec. and the negligibly small weight $w_c = 10^{-9}$ on the control activity.

A flow chart of the operations required every cycle in this second-order control computer program is shown in Fig. 4.5. The sequence of coefficients which must be placed in fixed storage for use by the second-order control computer program is shown in Table 4.2.

There is no assurance that this control program, which is optimal for the second-order simplified problem, can operate effectively in the third-order environment. To examine the performance of this trial second-order time-varying controller we evaluate its performance using the techniques of Chapter 2. We find that this control computer program succeeds in having a miss-distance of 24.8 ft. RMS with a peak acceleration of 345 ft. / sec.$^2$ RMS (satisfactorily below 400). If we compare this miss-distance with the bounds on the possible performance as summarized in Fig. 4.3, we see that this second-order controller outperforms the optimal third-order controller for $\Delta t = .8$ sec., which had a miss-distance of

Fig. 4.5 Flow Chart of the Operations Required Every Cycle in the Missile Second-Order Control Computer Program

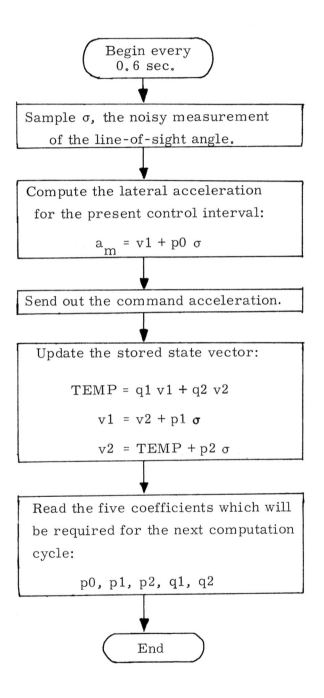

Table 4.2  The Sequence of Coefficients used by the Missile
Second-Order Control Computer Program

| Sample Instant | Time-To-Go | p0 | p1 | p2 | q1 | q2 |
|---|---|---|---|---|---|---|
| 1 | 12.0 | 0 | 0 | 0 | -.611 | 1.252 |
| 2 | 11.4 | 5222 | 1475 | -8 | -.279 | .984 |
| 3 | 10.8 | 5068 | 1178 | -276 | -.297 | 1.045 |
| 4 | 10.2 | 3811 | 842 | -472 | -.375 | 1.136 |
| 5 | 9.6 | 3142 | 598 | -664 | -.438 | 1.193 |
| 6 | 9.0 | 2973 | 443 | -839 | -.460 | 1.195 |
| 7 | 8.4 | 3104 | 334 | -1006 | -.449 | 1.159 |
| 8 | 7.8 | 3376 | 224 | -1187 | -.425 | 1.108 |
| 9 | 7.2 | 3689 | 79 | -1396 | -.401 | 1.054 |
| 10 | 6.6 | 4009 | -122 | -1641 | -.379 | .997 |
| 11 | 6.0 | 4349 | -399 | -1925 | -.356 | .934 |
| 12 | 5.4 | 4738 | -779 | -2245 | -.332 | .858 |
| 13 | 4.8 | 5206 | -1311 | -2592 | -.305 | .765 |
| 14 | 4.2 | 5780 | -2078 | -2925 | -.273 | .646 |
| 15 | 3.6 | 6500 | -3225 | -3119 | -.236 | .489 |
| 16 | 3.0 | 7426 | -5026 | -2801 | -.194 | .270 |
| 17 | 2.4 | 8664 | -8053 | -713 | -.143 | -.065 |
| 18 | 1.8 | 10397 | -13685 | 8484 | -.085 | -.684 |
| 19 | 1.2 | 13000 | -26309 | 0 | 0 | 0 |
| 20 | 0.6 | 17405 | 0 | 0 | 0 | 0 |

31. 3 ft. RMS. At the sample interval of $\Delta t = .6$ little can be done to improve the performance of the second-order controller because the theoretical measurement-limited optimal still would have a miss-distance of 23. 1 ft. RMS. Further improvement in performance, if any, must be gained by reducing the order of the controller still further and shortening the sample period in an attempt to approach more closely the lower bound given by the optimal continuous controller of about 14 ft. RMS.

## 4.4  The Design of Constant-Coefficient Controllers Using the Algorithms for Optimal Synthesis

Thus far the limits imposed by computer capacity have been related to the computer arithmetic speed.    Other computer limitations exist and must also be considered by the designer.  One such limitation is the size of the memory of the computer.  The time-varying control laws suggested by optimal control theory can require very large amounts of fixed memory to store the sequence of optimal coefficients.  Rarely does a control computer have unlimited storage capacity.  Memory blocks in the high-speed random access memory are rationed out to the various users who are programming the time-shared activities of the control computer.  Perhaps an auxiliary storage unit can be added to the computer for the purpose of storing the fixed sequence of coefficients for the controller.  A medium-speed sequentially storing device such as a magnetic drum or disc or tape would be satisfactory; the read-out of the coefficients in real time can be synchronized with the control activity.  Such an addition, however, might not be practical within the limits imposed by delivery schedules or unit costs or reliability.  Therefore the control system designer might prefer to simplify his theoretically optimal control program to enable him to pack it into the limited storage capacity already available.

One method of reducing the storage required by an optimal time-varying control program would be to fit easily computed functions to the sequences of gains.  The modified control computer program would then reconstruct the sequences by evaluating the functions in real time.  This would eliminate the bulk storage problem, although additional computation time would be required for the function evaluations.  The choice of functions with which to represent the gain sequences should be motivated by the nature of the actual optimal sequences. After producing a good match for the gain sequences, the performance of the modified design should be verified by the evaluation technique of Chapter 2.

In some applications a constant gain controller may be a very good approximation to the optimal controller. If the plant is not time-varying and if the statistics of the plant disturbances and measurement noises are stationary, then for computation times sufficiently after the initial time, optimal estimator gains settle down to constant values, independent of the initial state uncertainties. If in addition the cost weighting matrices are not time-varying, then for computation times sufficiently before the terminal time, optimal controller gains are constant, independent of the penalty to be placed on the terminal state. Thus for a sufficiently long operating period there exists a middle interval of time in which neither the estimator gains nor the controller gains are varying. That is, the optimal controller during this period of regulation is realized by a constant-coefficient control computer program. A practical control program could use the optimal regulator gains over the entire operating period, and in some applications the loss of optimality might not be too great.

The design of regulators to minimize a mean-squared error criterion in steady-state operation has been solved earlier in the literature by other means. Franklin (1955) and Chang (1958) used transfer functions and spectral factorization to solve a Wiener-Hopf equation. Thus they derived the optimum sampled-data controller for a plant subject to random inputs. Spectral factorization is not easy to perform numerically. Further, this work in its most direct form is restricted to single-input and single-output systems, and the plant must have all its poles and zeros inside the unit circle.

The procedure for generating an optimal time-varying controller according to the Joseph and Tou theory has many advantages over the earlier work involving spectral factorization. The recursive algorithms for generating the estimator or the controller are admirably suited to machine computation. The theory is not restricted to single-input and single-output systems. No mention is made about pole or zero locations. A nonminimum-phase plant or an unstable plant does not require special treatment.

As an example of the use of these algorithms to design an efficient constant-coefficient controller we consider part of the Apollo spacecraft control problem discussed in Appendix A. Suppose one wishes to design an attitude control autopilot to operate on the measured attitude error and produce commands to the nozzle angle actuator. For this demonstration we will not consider the offset angle of the center of mass and the lateral velocity of the vehicle. We will include the state variables associated with rigid rotation $(\omega, \theta)$, the first bending mode $(v_b, q)$, and the nozzle actuator lag $(\delta)$. The angular velocity $\omega$ of the rigid vehicle is governed by

$$\frac{d}{dt} \omega = - \frac{T}{I} [L \sigma_T + d_T] q(t) + \frac{T}{I} L [\delta(t) + n_T(t)] \tag{4.22}$$

where T is the thrust of the gimballed main engine, I is the pitch moment-of-inertia of the rigid vehicle, L is the distance from the engine gimbal to the vehicle center-of-mass, q is the generalized coordinate of the bending mode, $d_T$ and $\sigma_T$ are the displacement and slope of the bending mode at the thrust station per unit of the generalized coordinate, $\delta$ is the nonrandom part of the angle of the thrust vector with respect to the tail of the vehicle, and $n_T$ is the random part of that angle (assumed to be a white noise). The attitude commanded by the guidance is actually stepwise constant. At a relatively slower repetition rate the steering-control computer program processes the velocity measurements and produces new attitude commands. The attitude command is stepped suddenly to the new value and is then held constant until the next evaluation of the steering law. To model in a simple fashion the discontinuous nature of the attitude command, we will assume that the attitude command is the integral of a white noise $n_c(t)$. The attitude error $\theta$ of the rigid vehicle is then governed by

$$\frac{d}{dt} \theta = \omega(t) - n_c(t) \tag{4.23}$$

The spectral density of the noise $n_c$ is assumed to be .001 radians$^2$ per sec. This implies, for example, that in 10 sec. the attitude command will have wandered a RMS distance of .1 radian. The velocity $v_b$ of the generalized coordinate of the bending mode is governed by

91

$$\frac{d}{dt} v_b = - \omega_b^2 q(t) - \frac{T}{M} d_T [\delta(t) + n_T(t)] \qquad (4.24)$$

where $\omega_b$ is the natural radian frequency of the bending mode and M is the mass of the vehicle. The generalized coordinate q of the bending mode is governed by

$$\frac{d}{dt} q = v_b(t) \qquad (4.25)$$

Note we have assumed the bending mode has no damping. The nonrandom part $\delta$ of the angle of the thrust vector is governed by

$$\frac{d}{dt} \delta = \frac{1}{\tau} [\delta_c - \delta(t)] \qquad (4.26)$$

where $\tau$ is the lag of the nozzle actuator and $\delta_c$ is the nozzle angle to be commanded by the control program of the guidance computer.

The data available to the control program is a noisy and bent measurement e of the attitude error

$$e(t) = \theta(t) + \sigma_a q(t) + w(t) \qquad (4.27)$$

where $\sigma_a$ is the slope of the bending mode at the attitude read-out station and w is a random noise in the measurement related to the attitude quantization size. The control program samples the attitude error every $\Delta t$ seconds. Based upon all the measurements up to and including the present measurement, the control program computes and sends out the best nozzle angle command $\delta_c$. The nozzle angle command is held constant until the next computation.

The best control program is defined to be the linear constant coefficient control program which minimizes the mean value of the quadratic cost function. We must place into the cost function all quantities of interest which are to be held small through control action. These include attitude error, vehicle angular velocity, and bending energy. In addition a penalty must be placed on control activity so that the nozzle commands will not exceed the limits of the actuator. The cost function used in this demonstration is

92

$$\text{cost} = \frac{1}{T} \int_0^T \left[ \frac{1}{2} I \omega_{BW}^2 \, \theta^2 + \frac{1}{2} I \omega^2 + \frac{1}{2} M \omega_b^2 q^2 + \frac{1}{2} M v_b^2 + W \dot{\delta}^2 \right] dt$$

(4.28)

The second term in the integrand is the kinetic energy of the vehicle due to rigid rotation $\omega$. The third term is the potential energy due to the bending coordinate $q$. The fourth term is the kinetic energy due to the bending velocity $v_b$. The first term is the penalty placed on attitude error $\theta$. This term differs from the second term by the introduction of a weighting number $\omega_{BW}$. The assignment of a value to $\omega_{BW}$ determines approximately the radian frequency bandwidth of the resulting design. We will use a value for $\omega_{BW}$ of 1 radian per sec. The last term is a penalty placed on nozzle rate $\dot{\delta}$. A reasonable choice for the weight W may be motivated as follows: In this problem we actually must constrain both the nozzle rate and the bending energy. The nozzle has a maximum rate capability of .1 radian/sec. The docking tunnel may break if the bending coordinate reaches .1 ft. Thus for safety and to assure that the autopilot performs as designed using the linear theory, the RMS values of both quantities should be held below their limits. It often turns out that the optimal design is such that the mean value of the control activity penalty term is nearly equal to the sum of the mean values of the terms being regulated. Also the individual terms being regulated may be nearly equal. With four terms being regulated, let us assume then that the mean value of the weighted nozzle activity will equal four times the mean value of the mean bending potential energy

$$E[W \dot{\delta}^2] = 4 E[\frac{1}{2} M \omega_b^2 q^2]$$

(4.29)

A possible choice of the weight W is then

$$W = \frac{2 M \omega_b^2 q_{max}^2}{\dot{\delta}_{max}^2}$$

(4.30)

93

where $q_{max}$ is the maximum permissible value of the bending coordinate and $\delta_{max}$ is the maximum rate capability of the nozzle. This choice implies that we want the optimal design to perform with the mean-square bending coordinate and the mean-square nozzle rate similar percentages below their maximum permissible levels. According to Eq. (4.30) we will use a value for W of $4.4 \times 10^5$.

We write a simple main program which incorporates the mathematical description of the continuous stochastic problem as given above. Then using the general-purpose subroutines described in Appendix C, the main program calls for the design of the optimal controller: Program SAMPL-SETUP converts the vehicle differential equations and the continuous cost functional into the equivalent state transition and discrete cost function formulation. Given the sampled formulation of the vehicle dynamics and the statistics of the disturbances driving the process, program ESTIMA-TOR is used to find the steady-state optimal filter gains. Given the sampled formulation of the vehicle dynamics and the cost function, program CONTROLLER is used to find the steady-state optimal controller gains. The estimator and controller are combined into a state space representation which is then transformed into canonical form yielding a minimum arithmetic control computer program. Finally so that the design engineer can evaluate the performance of the control program, the root-mean-square values of all the quantities of interest are computed, using program EVALUATOR.

Using the numerical values for the vehicle and cost parameters as described above and in Appendix A, we asked the automated design package to design the optimal control program for a sample period of $\Delta t = .1$ sec. The resulting control program is

$$\delta_{c_i} = x1_i + po\ e_i$$

$$
\begin{bmatrix} x1_{i+1} \\ x2_{i+1} \\ x3_{i+1} \\ x4_{i+1} \\ x5_{i+1} \end{bmatrix}
=
\begin{bmatrix}
0 & 1 & 0 & 0 & 0 \\
0 & 0 & 1 & 0 & 0 \\
0 & 0 & 0 & 1 & 0 \\
0 & 0 & 0 & 0 & 1 \\
q1 & q2 & q3 & q4 & q5
\end{bmatrix}
\begin{bmatrix} x1_i \\ x2_i \\ x3_i \\ x4_i \\ x5_i \end{bmatrix}
+
\begin{bmatrix} p1 \\ p2 \\ p3 \\ p4 \\ p5 \end{bmatrix}
e_i \quad (4.31)
$$

with

$$p0 = -.20305$$

| | |
|---|---|
| $p1 = -.05831$ | $q1 = 0.0002$ |
| $p2 = -.08961$ | $q2 = -0.7044$ |
| $p3 = -.11167$ | $q3 = 2.3903$ |
| $p4 = -.08364$ | $q4 = -3.4927$ |
| $p5 = -.01578$ | $q5 = 2.7819$ |

The control program takes the i-th measurement $e_i$, performs one multiply and one add, and immediately sends out the i-th nozzle command $\delta_{c_i}$. Then the control program prepares for the next measurement time by performing the indicated state update.

The optimal control program operating in the assumed stochastic environment produces the following root-mean-square values for quantities of interest in the vehicle: attitude error 4.3 degrees, rigid vehicle angular velocity 2.4 degrees per sec., bending coordinate .06 feet, bending coordinate velocity .6 feet per sec., nozzle angular velocity 4.1 degrees per sec., and nozzle angle 1.5 degrees. The penalty weight placed on nozzle rate appears to be appropriate, as the resulting theoretical nozzle activity of the optimal design falls within both the angular rate capability and the angular excursion capability of the actual nozzle. Also the bending coordinate is below its tolerable limit.

To increase our understanding of how the optimal digital program controls the vehicle, it is useful to consider the frequency domain (z-transform properties of the vehicle and optimal compensation. We convert the state space representations to z-transforms, and then factor the numerator and denominator polynomials to determine the zeros and poles of the system. Several subroutines by Fraser (1965) were very helpful in performing these calculations.

The zeros and poles of the vehicle transfer function (from nozzle command to attitude error) are shown in Fig. 4.6. The zeros and poles of the autopilot transfer function (from attitude error to nozzle command) are shown in Fig. 4.7. The roots of the closed-loop system are shown in Fig. 4.8. The optimal compensation has a zero just to the left of $z = 1$; this stabilizes the double pole of the rigid rotation mode. Behind this low-frequency zero are two poles; these poles serve to reduce the high-frequency

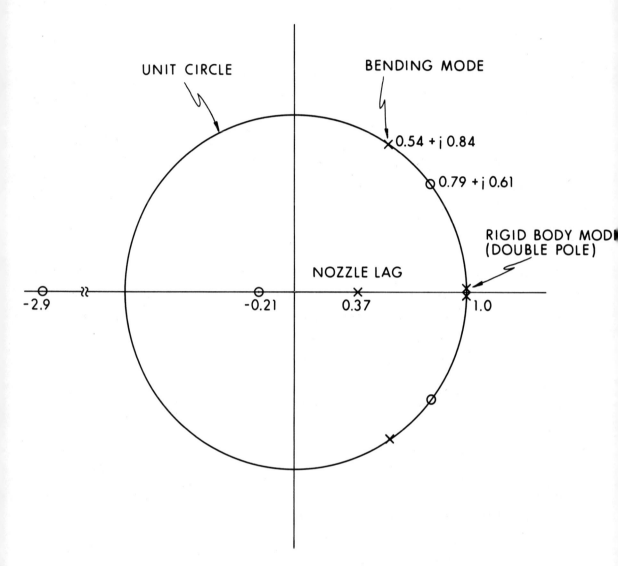

Fig. 4.6    Vehicle Dynamics; Pole-Zero Locations in the Z-Plane

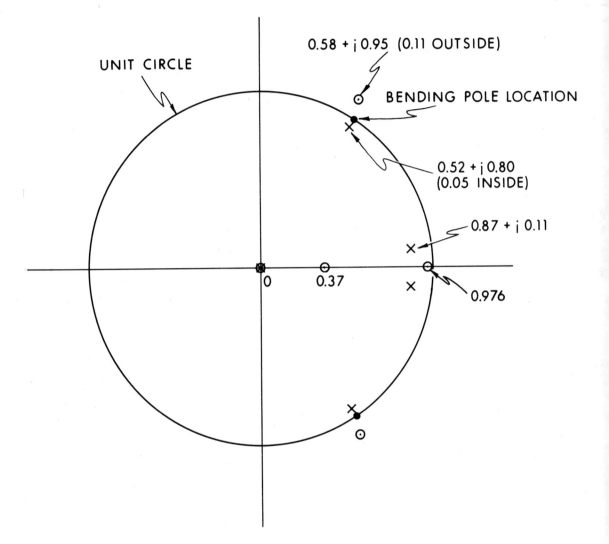

Fig. 4.7    Optimal Autopilot; Pole-Zero Locations in the Z-Plane

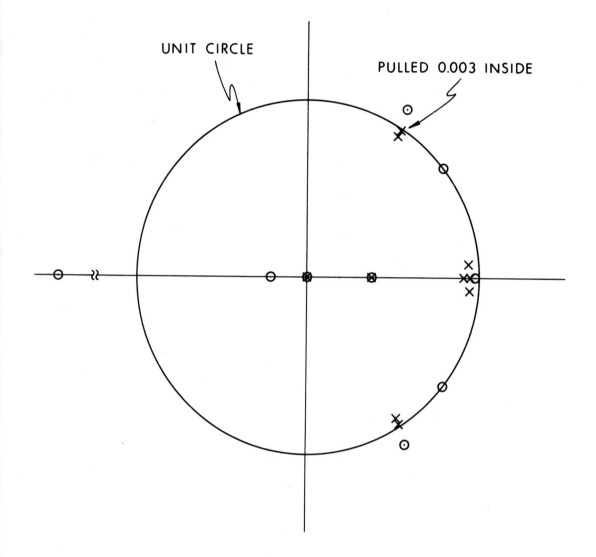

Fig. 4.8   Closed-Loop Dynamics of Autopilot and Vehicle; Pole-
Zero Locations in the Z-Plane

gain of the compensation, thus reducing the transmission of the noise. All this low-frequency compensation results in a phase relationship at the bending frequency which would cause a bending mode instability. However, the optimal compensation quite cleverly places a compensation pole inside and a compensation zero outside the vehicle bending pole. This causes almost no gain variation but reverses the phase about $180^{\circ}$ at the bending frequency, thus stabilizing the bending mode. This aspect of the optimal design was a total surprise to all of us who have looked at the Apollo autopilot design problem. None of us had considered the possible use of nonminimum-phase complex zeros to achieve a desired gain or phase characteristic. In fact, a result of root locus theory is that for infinite closed-loop gain, poles move to the zero locations. Therefore in a cut-and-try design procedure, the designer instinctively places compensation zeros inside the unit circle. The optimal design in this demonstration points out that this is an unnecessary inhibition.

One pole of the optimal autopilot was located at $z = .00027$. One zero was located at $z = .00038$. One can most surely cancel this pole-zero pair which is internal to the autopilot. This would reduce the order of the autopilot to fourth order. The reason for the existence of a pole-zero pair which nearly cancels is probably related to the very small measurement noise. In general if a measurement is noise-free, then the optimal estimator is of lower order than otherwise required.

A disadvantage of the theoretically optimal design is that if the actual bending frequency of the vehicle differs from the value assumed for the purpose of design, then the closed-loop operation may be unstable. This is a recurring shortcoming of many optimal design approaches; the theoretically optimal design may be too highly tuned to the mathematical values assumed for key vehicle parameters. This problem will be discussed in the concluding chapter.

Truncation has been a problem in implementing digital autopilots (see Stubbs (1965), Martin (1965b), and Whitman (1966)). The Apollo guidance computer has a word-length or single-precision accuracy of about four decimal digits. Martin showed that for one proposed autopilot design, if the coefficients in the indicated control program were rounded to four digits, then some of the compensation poles jumped outside the unit circle. Thus double-precision arithmetic has to be considered to guarantee the stability of the compensation.

We have repeated this truncation test on the optimal design. The delightful result is that rounding all coefficients to four digits produced no significant shift in any zeros or poles. For example, the largest shift was shown by the low-frequency complex pole pair: it moved from $z = .8727 \pm j.1103$ to $z = .8726 \pm j.1114$, a shift of 1%.

It is interesting to speculate that low sensitivity to truncation may be a general property of optimal digital control programs. By the definition of optimality, the optimal program minimizes the cost. The cost can be considered a measure of the stability of the design. Thus for an optimal design, a small first-order change in the control program (such as that due to truncation) should produce only a second-order change in the related stability.

Additional insight into the nature of optimal controllers can be gained by eliminating certain disturbances from the original problem statement. We have, for example, designed the optimal controller for an identical process but with no thrust vibration noise disturbing the vehicle. The poles and zeros of this autopilot are shown in Fig. 4.9. This theoretically optimal controller is completely impractical. It uses cancellation compensation and places a zero at exactly $z = 1.0$. The steady-state gain of this autopilot is zero, so the vehicle can be pointed with any arbitrary steady attitude error and the controller will take no action. Optimal control theory takes at face value the exact problem statement. In this case we said that there were no disturbances driving the vehicle, so the optimal controller concludes that vehicle attitude can be exactly inferred from the known dynamics of the vehicle in response to the known sequence of nozzle commands. It in effect ignores the feedback measurement of attitude. Cancellation compensation is also used for the bending mode. A compensation zero is placed exactly on the (supposedly) known location of the bending pole. The optimal controller seems to believe that if it sends out no signal at the bending frequency, then no energy can get into the bending mode.

In an alternate example we have designed the optimal compensation for a process with the thrust vibration restored but with the attitude command motion set to zero. The poles and zeros of the resulting design are shown in Fig. 4.10. This design is a higher gain design than the original optimal design shown in Fig. 4.7. With no random walk component in the

100

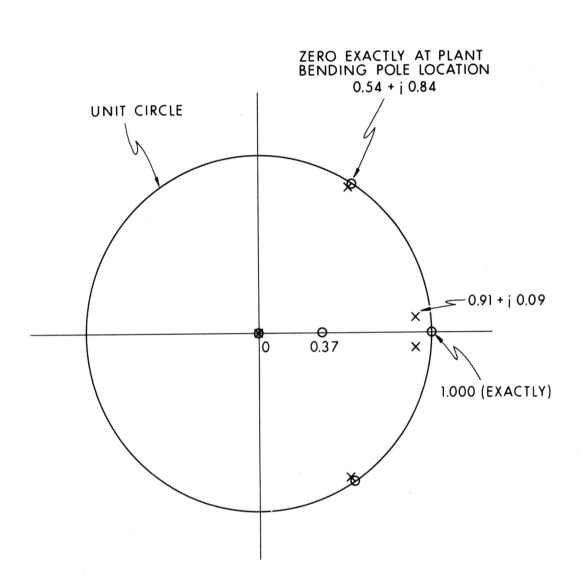

Fig. 4.9 Optimal Autopilot if the Thrust Vibration Is Assumed to Be Zero; Cancellation Compensation

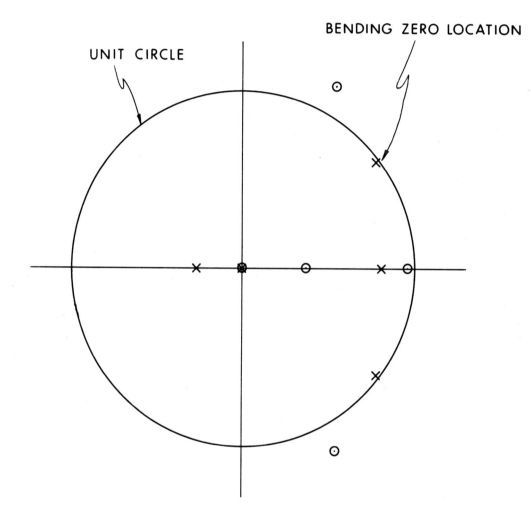

Fig. 4.10  Optimal Autopilot if the Attitude Command Is
Assumed Held Constant

error signal, the optimal controller assumes that the error signal is dominated by the bending dynamics. It feels free to place a pole almost at the unit circle exactly at the location of the bending zero. This would have the unfortunate effect that with the actual broad-band content of the discontinuous attitude command signal, this lightly damped compensation mode would be excited and would produce useless oscillatory nozzle command signals.

It is clear that one must be careful in developing the mathematical description of a problem to be solved by optimal control theory. The optimal design will use every bit of information quite literally, whether or not this is actually practical. We have seen the advantage of examining the frequency domain representation of a constant-coefficient optimal design as it shows clearly some shortcomings of the design which may not be evident in the time domain. Also the frequency domain representation suggested a reduction in the order of the optimal controller.

# Chapter 5

## The Optimization of Simplified Controller Designs

### 5.1  Introduction

The design philosophy of Phillips (James, Nichols, and Phillips
(1947)) is a practical method for optimizing a simplified controller design.  One leaves as undetermined certain parameters in the trial controller design.  The mean quadratic cost of operating the process with
the trial controller is considered to be a function of the free parameters.
One then searches for the parameter values which will minimize the mean
cost function.  For the continuous stationary stochastic control problem
Phillips showed how the steady-state mean-squared error can be expressed
as an explicit function of the statistics of the noises, the statistics of the
desired output, the fixed parameters in the plant, and the fixed and free
parameters in the trial controller.

Robinson (1957) applied this design philosophy to sampled-data
stationary stochastic control problems.  Without the aid of high-speed
digital computers neither Phillips nor Robinson could demonstrate the
method for complicated processes.  A typical example by Robinson was
to find the best zero-order constant-coefficient controller (a simple gain)
when the plant was only of first order.  The solution was obtained analytically, not numerically.  No discussion was given of how the method
could be applied to a design problem of a realistic order.

Johansen (1964) extended the design philosophy to nonstationary
stochastic continuous controllers.  In a major departure from the methods
used by Phillips or Robinson, Johansen computed the mean cost of a trial
design using time-domain and state-space techniques, rather than fre-
quency-domain and transform techniques.  Johansen then developed a
computational procedure for iteratively converging to the time-variation
of the gains required to minimize the mean cost.

In this chapter we continue the work of Phillips, Robinson, and

Johansen.  In particular we will focus our attention on non-stationary sampled-data controllers.  In Chapter 2 we showed how to compute the mean quadratic cost of operating a linear plant with any given linear sampled-data controller.  If the design engineer leaves as undetermined certain parameters in his assumed structure of the controller, then the computations define the mean quadratic cost as a function of these undetermined parameters.  In Section 5.2 we discuss certain problems in choosing a controller structure having a limited number of undetermined parameters.  In Section 5.3 we review techniques available for finding the minimum of a function.  We discuss the application of the Davidon descent method to the determination of the best values for the free parameters.  In Section 5.4 we provide two design examples: the design of an optimized time-varying cross-product steering law and the design of the best constant-coefficient first-order controller for the air-to-air missile.  We conclude the chapter in Section 5.5 with a general discussion of other promising minimization algorithms.

## 5.2    Choosing a Controller Structure with Limited Parameter Time-Varying Gains

Johansen considered the problem of optimizing the time-variation of the gains in a continuous stochastic controller.  The design engineer would specify the structure of the controller, including the dimension of the controller state space and the coefficients which would be permitted to be nonzero.  Then Johansen provided a numerical procedure for converging to the time-variation of the nonzero gains which minimizes the mean quadratic cost.  Johansen illustrated his design procedure by synthesizing a continuous time-varying controller for the air-to-air missile problem.  (This problem is also used by us and is described in Appendix B.)

In the design illustration, Johansen encountered one disappointing result: the method would converge to different time-variations for the gains depending on his initial choice of time-variation used to start the iterative procedure.  In each case the design converged to the same minimum value for the cost, but the controller would be somewhat different.  Johansen ascribed the difficulty to two possible sources: First, the state space representation which was assumed for the controller was too general.  A transformation of the state space of the controller could lead to a different controller having the same input-output transmission. Thus the minimization problem as formulated did not have a unique solution.  Second, the state space representation for the continuous controller necessarily included a feedback matrix from controller state to controller state derivative.  High-frequency time-variations in the elements of this feedback matrix were poorly determined by the iterative procedure.  The cost is a function of the controller output signal, which is a function of the controller state vector.  But the controller state vector is influenced by the feedback of its state through integration.  The integration attentuates the effect of any high-frequency variations in the feedback gains. The higher the frequency, the greater is the attenuation.  Thus the cost is relatively insensitive to high-frequency variations in the elements of the feedback matrix.

Building on Johansen's experience the design engineer should keep in mind two suggestions:  First, in assuming a structure for the controller one should limit himself to a canonical form state space representation.  This provides a unique solution to the optimization problem. As a bonus in the computer controller application the resulting control program will require only the minimum amount of arithmetic.  Second, rather than permit a free variation in the time-varying coefficients, the designer should limit the possible variation to that generated by simple functions with undetermined parameters.  This eliminates the possibility of useless high-frequency variations appearing in the gains.  And by replacing the search of infinite function space with a search of a finite parameter space, the digital computer time required to find the minimum cost design is reduced.

Johansen did not discuss methods for approximating the arbitrary time-variations for the gains found to be optimal.  In synthesizing the gains using analogue equipment some degree of approximation must be used if the design is to be practical.  The performance of the approximate synthesis should be evaluated to ensure that the performance has not been seriously degraded.

To avoid numerical difficulties we suggested that the possible variations in the gains should be limited to that generated by simple functions with undetermined parameters.  This can have an additional benefit if the simple functions are easily synthesized in the analogue case or are easily computed in real time in the digital case: The approximation problem has been eliminated. One can implement directly the optimized gain functions of time. Some examples of easily computed gain variations are: piecewise constant gains, piecewise linear gains, polynominal gains, rational gains, or exponential gains.

To be practical the design engineer must recognize that the numerical search of the parameter space for the minimum cost design will be a slow (costly) process if many parameters in the design are left unspecified. Therefore one should devote considerable attention toward developing a trial controller structure that is likely to be effective. Often a good trial structure can be suggested by solving analytically a simpler problem. Analytical solutions when obtainable give valuable insight into the relationships between process and optimal controller parameters. Alternately a good trial structure might be suggested by developing numerically the Joseph and Tou controller for the full problem or a simpler problem. By looking at the time variation of the optimal gain sequences, efficient approximating functions might become obvious.

Perhaps a trial-and-error or other design approach has already found a reasonable controller design. This design can be improved by optimizing parameters by the method of this chapter.

The design effort need not be completed in one step. One might attempt a systematic reduction to lower-order controllers or to less complicated gain variations. The optimized design found at one stage would suggest simplified trial structures for the next stage. With only modest simplifications at each stage, it is more likely that nearly optimal performance can be maintained while working toward a simplified controller.

## 5.3 An Automatic Search for the Best Values for the Undetermined Parameters

To make practical the optimization procedure, one must devote considerable attention to the efficiency of the method used to conduct the numerical search for the minimum cost design. Two areas should be considered: the computation of the mean cost as a function of a given choice for the set of parameters, and the descent method used to find the minimum of the cost function.

108

In Chapter 2 we derived a recursive formula for computing the mean cost of operating a given controller. The formula used a sampled representation of the continuous stochastic process. In many applications much of the stochastic environment is stationary including the dynamics of the plant. It is possible that key arrays in the sampled-data formulation, such as the state-transition matrix of the plant, need be computed by integration only once. The resulting values hold true for all sample intervals. In these applications the discrete recursive formula for computing the cost is much more efficient than an equivalent formulation which would compute the cost by integration throughout the entire operating period.

The most time-consuming portion of the recursive formula for evaluating the cost is Eq. (2.86), which computes the covariance of the combined plant and controller state space. The multiplication of two square matrices of dimension n requires $n^3$ scalar multiplications. Thus the time required to compute the cost grows as the cube of the dimension of the combined plant and controller state space. Clearly it is advisable at the outset to make all reasonable simplifications in the mathematical model for the process. A problem with half as many state variables can be evaluated eight times as fast. Also the time required to compute the cost grows directly with the length of the operating period. Thus one should assume the shortest operating period which is still able to demonstrate the nonstationary aspects of the control problem.

Having formulated the optimization problem efficiently, one then considers numerical methods for finding the values of the free parameters which will minimize the cost function. The simplest method is an exhaustive evaluation of points throughout the parameter space. Suppose there are two free parameters, and the best values for the parameters can reasonably be expected to lie between 0 and 1. If we wish to know the location of the minimum to an accuracy of the order of .1, then we should examine 10 values of the first variable (spaced .1 apart) for each of 10 values of the second variable (also spaced .1 apart). Thus we would compute the cost at 100 points in the variable space and would assume the location of the lowest value discovered was close to the true minimum. But if we wanted an accuracy ten times more refined, this would require a one-hundred-fold increase in the number of points to be evaluated; that is, an accuracy of .01 would require 10,000 points. The growth in the required number of points is even more severe for higher-dimensional spaces. Thus direct search techniques become completely impractical if the minimum must be located to within small tolerances. On the other hand, an exhaustive search has some important advantages: One can estimate beforehand the amount of computer time that will be required to complete the fixed search pattern. Also a direct search can locate the true minimum; it will not converge to a point which is only a local relative minimum.

An increase in efficiency can be gained by using a gradient technique. If one can calculate the gradient of the function with respect to the variables, then one can step in the direction of steepest descent until the minimum is reached. A survey of some of the gradient techniques is provided by Spang (1962). A problem in applying the method of steepest descent is the choice of the step size to be taken in the indicated direction. If the step size is too small, then little progress will be made toward the minimum. If the step size is too large, then the minimum may be over-stepped. One can avoid this problem by performing a one-dimensional search for a minimum along the straight line indicated by the last computation of the gradient. When the minimum along the line is found, a new gradient is calculated at that point. The method continues by looking for the minimum in the direction indicated by the new gradient.

A numerical difficulty frequently will occur, when applying the method of linear minimizations, with new directions selected by the gradient. For example, in two-dimensional space, the function may have a long valley with steep walls but a gently sloping bottom. If one searches in a fixed direction until a minimum has been found, the new gradient at the minimum will be at right angles to the previous search direction. Thus the second search direction is perpendicular to the first. And the third is perpendicular to the second, which makes the third direction parallel to the first direction. Thus the directions of search become fixed by the initial gradient direction. If the floor of the valley happened to be oriented halfway between the two gradient directions, then the minimization procedure would oscillate back and forth between the two valley walls making only slow progress toward the true minimum during each iteration.

A more powerful method which overcomes the difficulties of the previous methods is the generalized Newton-Raphson iteration. (General references include Householder (1953) and Traub (1964)). Here one takes advantage of not only the gradient of the function but also the curvature. Thus the method automatically can estimate the direction to the minimum as well as the distance to the minimum. At the minimum, knowledge of the curvature of the function provides valuable information about how sharp or broad is the minimum. The method can exhibit rapid convergence to the minimum, if the function has quadratic behavior at the minimum. Consider an n-dimensional quadratic function having a minimum of $f_0$ at the point $\underline{x}_0$:

$$f(\underline{x}) = f_0 + \frac{1}{2} (\underline{x} - \underline{x}_0)^T J (\underline{x} - \underline{x}_0) \qquad (5.1)$$

where J is the matrix of second partial derivatives

$$J_{ij} = \frac{\partial^2 f}{\partial x_i \, \partial x_j} \qquad (5.2)$$

whose elements are independent of $\underline{x}$. The gradient of the quadratic function at an arbitrary point $\underline{x}$ is

$$\underline{g}(\underline{x}) = J (\underline{x} - \underline{x}_0) \qquad (5.3)$$

One may solve for the location $\underline{x}_0$ of the minimum in terms of the gradient at $\underline{x}$ and the matrix of second partials J

$$\underline{x}_0 = \underline{x} - J^{-1} \underline{g}(\underline{x}) \qquad (5.4)$$

Equation (5.4) is an explicit formula for locating the minimum of the quadratic function. (It should be pointed out that in general Eq. (5.4) brings you to the stationary point of the quadratic, where the gradient is zero. This may or may not be a minimum depending on whether or not the matrix J is positive definite.)

Equation (5.4) suggests an iterative procedure which may be used to find the minimum of an analytic but nonquadratic function:

$$\underline{x}_{i+1} = \underline{x}_i - J(\underline{x}_i)^{-1} \underline{g}(\underline{x}_i) \qquad (5.5)$$

111

One must compute the gradient of the function at the point $\underline{x}_i$ (the vector of first partials) and the Jacobian of the function also at the point $\underline{x}_i$ (the matrix of second partials). The estimate of the location of the minimum $\underline{x}_{i+1}$ is then computed from Eq. (5.5). One steps to the new point and repeats the procedure. It can be shown that the method has quadratic convergence. That is, sufficiently close to the minimum, the increase in the number of correct significant figures produced by applying Eq. (5.5) is double the increase produced by the previous iteration.

An alternate iterative procedure, also having quadratic convergence, was suggested by Davidon (1959). This procedure was further developed by Fletcher and Powell (1963). In this method the matrix J is not evaluated directly, and no matrix need be inverted. Instead a matrix H is used and an estimate of the total step required to reach the minimum is given as

$$\underline{s}_i = - H_i \, \underline{g}\,(\underline{x}_i) \tag{5.6}$$

One searches in the direction of $\underline{s}_i$ until a minimum is found at $\underline{x}_{i+1}$. One evaluates the gradient $\underline{g}\,(\underline{x}_{i+1})$ at the new point. The matrix H is then modified as an explicit function of the last directed step and the resulting change in the gradient:

$$\underline{\sigma}_i = \underline{x}_{i+1} - \underline{x}_i \tag{5.7}$$

$$\underline{y}_i = \underline{g}\,(\underline{x}_{i+1}) - \underline{g}\,(\underline{x}_i) \tag{5.8}$$

$$H_{i+1} = H_i + \frac{\underline{\sigma}_i \, \underline{\sigma}_i^{\,T}}{\underline{\sigma}_i^{\,T} \, \underline{y}_i} - \frac{H_i \, \underline{y}_i \, \underline{y}_i^{\,T} \, H_i}{\underline{y}_i^{\,T} \, H_i \, \underline{y}_i} \tag{5.9}$$

The procedure is repeated until the method converges to the minimum. It is shown that if the initial H matrix is chosen to be positive definite (such as $H_0 = I$), then the method is stable. That is, the direction given by Eq. (5.6) will always be downhill. Therefore a relative minimum can be found in that direction which is lower than the previous minimum. Also it is shown that the method will find the minimum of an n-dimensional quadratic in exactly n linear searches, and the matrix H will converge to the inverse $J^{-1}$ of the matrix of second partials.

We have applied the method of Davidon to our minimization

problems with good results. Program MINFINDER in Appendix C incorporates this method. Some practical details should be mentioned. First, the method of Davidon assumes that the analytical gradient of the function is available and is easily computed. Rather than derive the required analytical formulas for the components of the gradient of the cost function, we have chosen to estimate the gradient by taking appropriate differences between neighboring values of the cost. To illustrate the basic ideas, consider a function of two variables. The Taylor series expansion of the function about the point $\underline{x} = \underline{0}$ may be written

$$f(x_1, x_2) = c + g_1 x_1 + g_2 x_2 + \frac{1}{2} J_{11} x_1^2 + J_{12} x_1 x_2 + \frac{1}{2} J_{22} x_2^2$$
$$+ 0(x^3) \tag{5.10}$$

where $0(x^3)$ denotes terms of order three or higher. The first component of the gradient of the function at $x_1 = 0$ and $x_2 = 0$ may be computed analytically:

$$\left. \frac{\partial f}{\partial x_1} \right]_{\underline{x} = \underline{0}} = g_1 \tag{5.11}$$

We could estimate this component of the gradient by taking a difference suggested by the definition of the partial derivative.

$$\frac{1}{x_1} \left[ f(x_1, 0) - f(0, 0) \right] = \frac{1}{x_1} \left[ (c + g_1 x_1 + \frac{1}{2} J_{11} x_1^2) - (c) + 0(x^3) \right]$$
$$\tag{5.12}$$
$$= g_1 + \frac{1}{2} J_{11} x_1 + 0(x^2)$$

Equation (5.12) when compared with Eq. (5.11) shows that this finite difference formula is in error by an amount which is directly proportional to the size of the differencing interval $x_1$. The formula approaches the correct value for the derivative only in the limit as $x_1$ goes to zero. But one is prevented from choosing an arbitrarily small value for $x_1$ because of the limitations of floating decimal point arithmetic used by digital computers. The number of significant figures remaining in the difference between two nearly equal numbers can only be as great as the number of figures that were different in the original numbers. For example, if two ten-digit numbers differ only in the last three digits, then their difference will contain only three significant figures.

An alternate formula for estimating the first component of the gradient would use a balanced forward-backward difference:

$$\frac{1}{2x_1} \left[ f(x_1, 0) - f(-x_1, 0) \right] = \frac{1}{2x_1} \left[ (c + g_1 x_1 + \frac{1}{2} J_{11} x_1^2) - (c - g_1 x_1 + \frac{1}{2} J_{11} x_1^2) + 0(x^3) \right]$$

(5.13)

$$= g_1 + 0(x^2)$$

Equation (5.13) when compared with Eq. (5.11) shows that the balanced difference formula has an error only second order in the differencing interval $x_1$. Thus it may be possible to find a differencing interval sufficiently large to avoid the floating point truncation problem but sufficiently small so that the second-order error is negligible.

The discussion may be generalized easily to n-dimensional functions. The balanced forward-backward difference retains the property that the error is only of second order. In our computer program, which implements the Davidon method, we estimate the gradient using these balanced differences.

The method of Davidon requires that one find the minimum of the function along the line in a given direction. A method for finding this minimum was not central to his theory, so no discussion was given of efficient methods for finding this minimum. The method we have programmed proceeds in three stages: In the first stage we make use of the fact that Eq. (5.6) not only gives the direction of the line but also has a magnitude which is an estimate of the distance to the minimum. This provides the basis for the first trial step. However, in early iterations the matrix H will not be close to the inverse $J^{-1}$ of the matrix of second partials. Therefore, it is reasonable to limit the first trial step to one no larger than that required to reach the minimum of a parabola having the same value f and the same slope df/ds at the beginning of the line and having an estimated minimum value of $f_0$. Such a parabola is governed by the equation

$$f(s) - f_0 = \frac{1}{2} k (s - s_0)^2$$

(5.14)

The slope of the parabola is

$$\frac{df}{ds} = k \, (s - s_0)$$ 

(5. 15)

Equations (5. 14) and (5. 15) may be combined to eliminate the unavailable curvature k:

$$f\,(s) - f_0 = \frac{1}{2} \frac{df}{ds} \, (s - s_0)$$ 

(5. 16)

Thus in terms of the function value, derivative, and minimum value, the step required to reach the minimum from s = 0 is

$$s_0 = \frac{2\,(f - f_0)}{-\dfrac{df}{ds}}$$ 

(5. 17)

In the computer program, the function value f at the beginning of the line is available as the end point of the previous iteration. The directional derivative df/ds along the line may be computed as the dot product of the gradient with the unit vector along the line. The minimum value $f_0$ of the function in this direction is unknown and must be estimated. For a positive quadratic cost function a lower bound is always zero. A tighter lower bound may be available if one has already synthesized and evaluated the Joseph and Tou optimal stochastic controller. The cost using the optimal controller by definition is lower than the cost which will be found using another controller. One must be careful to use a value for $f_0$ which is indeed lower than the true minimum of the function. Otherwise imposing Eq. (5. 17), as a limit on the step size permitted in the first stage of each iteration, will prevent rapid convergence of the method, since the maximum permitted will be shorter than the full step required.

To guarantee the stability of the minimization, one does not accept a trial point as the basis for continuing the search unless the trial is successful. A successful trial is defined to be one where the value of the function is found to be lower than or equal to the previously known lowest value of the function. If the method for selecting the step size in the first stage fails to produce a success, we cut the trial step size by a factor of ten and try again. This retreat back toward the beginning of the line is repeated until a successful point is found. It is guaranteed that a success eventually will occur, because as mentioned before the line is directed downhill.

After the first stage of the iteration succeeds, we retain the successful point as well as the initial point. In the second stage we look for a third point. A search procedure which seems to work efficiently was suggested by Rosenbrock (1960). One first tries a step size which is triple the step size used in the previous success. If the initial trial is a success, we go on to the third stage of the iteration. But if the trial is a failure, one searches for a successful point in the vicinity of the last successful point by alternately looking ahead and behind the last point while cutting the trial step size in half. Eventually a successful point will be found.

Now one has a sequence of three points. In the third and successive stages we iterate to the minimum by using the last three successful points with parabolic interpolation to estimate the location of the minimum. Using Newton's interpolation formula with divided differences (see Householder (1953) or Hildebrand (1956)), one can compute the first and second divided differences as

$$\Delta 1\,(s_1, s_2) = \frac{f(s_1)}{s_1 - s_2} + \frac{f(s_2)}{s_2 - s_1} \tag{5.18}$$

$$\Delta 2\,(s_1, s_2, s_3) = \frac{f(s_1)}{(s_1 - s_2)(s_1 - s_3)} + \frac{f(s_2)}{(s_2 - s_1)(s_2 - s_3)} + \frac{f(s_3)}{(s_3 - s_1)(s_3 - s_2)} \tag{5.19}$$

The equation of the parabola passing through the three points in terms of the divided differences is

$$f(s) = f(s_1) + (s - s_1)\,\Delta 1 + (s - s_1)(s - s_2)\,\Delta 2 \tag{5.20}$$

The first derivative of the parabola is

$$\frac{df}{ds} = \Delta 1 + (2s - s_1 - s_2)\,\Delta 2 \tag{5.21}$$

If the second divided difference is positive, the parabola has a minimum where the first derivative is zero. In this case, the step required to reach the minimum of the parabola from the last point is

$$s_0 - s_1 = \frac{s_2 - s_1}{2} - \frac{\Delta 1}{2\,\Delta 2} \qquad (5.22)$$

Equations (5.18), (5.19), and (5.22) form the algorithm for selecting the next trial point in terms of the last three successful points. To keep the trial step reasonable, the indicated step is limited to triple the previous successful step. If the second divided difference is negative or zero (indicating a parabola concave downward or a straight line), the parabolic method is not used; the program goes back to the second stage to find a new successful point. When the parabolic method is used and the trial step is a failure, the program searches for a successful point as before by alternately looking ahead and behind the last successful point while cutting the trial step size in half.

The search for the minimum along the given line continues by repeated use of the parabolic interpolation, based on the latest three successful points. To terminate the search one must establish a rule for deciding when the minimum has been reached. One can select a small criterion number, and when the last successful step is smaller than this criterion number, it can be assumed that the minimum is nearby. In some cases, trial points will fail both ahead and behind the last successful point within the criterion distance. This is definite proof that the minimum lies within the criterion distance. Our minimization program terminates the linear search when either one of these conditions is met.

The minimization program assumes that the minimum in n-dimensional space has been found if the last linear search involved a total step, from the beginning of the line to the minimum, no larger than the criterion number. Also in cases of slow convergence it may be necessary to stop the program at some maximum number of calls to the function to limit the use of computer time.

As a demonstration of the Davidon minimization method, we can search for the minimum of an interesting test function, proposed by Rosenbrock (1960):

$$f(x_1, x_2) = 100\,(x_2 - x_1^2)^2 + (1 - x_1)^2 \qquad (5.23)$$

117

This has a minimum value f = 0 at $x_1$ = $x_2$ = 1, with a curved valley following the parabola $x_2$ = $x_1^2$. The computer run is to be started from $x_1$ = - 1.2, $x_2$ = 1, so that the current point has to descend into the valley, and then follow it around the curve to the point (1, 1). The initial value of the estimate H of the inverse of the matrix of second partials is set as the identity matrix. Therefore the first iteration is in the direction of steepest descent. A value which works well for the differencing interval used to estimate the gradient was found to be $10^{-4}$. A good criterion number used to terminate the linear searches and the entire run was also $10^{-4}$. The lower bound on the function value is chosen to be zero. The current point at the end of each iteration is shown in Fig. 5.1. Near the end of the run, the method converges rapidly to an accurate estimate of the minimum value and its location. The following table summarizes the terminal iterations of the program:

| iteration | $f(x_1, x_2)$ | $x_1$ | $x_2$ | function evaluations |
|---|---|---|---|---|
| 16 | $2.6 \times 10^{-2}$ | .861 | .732 | 225 |
| 17 | $1.3 \times 10^{-3}$ | .979 | .955 | 241 |
| 18 | $6.7 \times 10^{-4}$ | .974 | .949 | 250 |
| 19 | $1.5 \times 10^{-5}$ | .9992 | .9980 | 260 |
| 20 | $8.5 \times 10^{-7}$ | .9991 | .9982 | 269 |
| 21 | $4.2 \times 10^{-11}$ | .9999993 | .9999992 | 279 |
| 22 | $3.4 \times 10^{-12}$ | .999998 | .999996 | 287 |

The method was quite close to the true location of the minimum after the 21st iteration, but the total step size exceeded $10^{-4}$. Therefore one more iteration took place. In this last iteration the step size was smaller than $10^{-4}$, so the run terminated. The last estimate H of the of the matrix of second partials (after the 21st iteration) was

$$H_{21} = \begin{bmatrix} .4996 & .9987 \\ .9987 & 2.0014 \end{bmatrix} \tag{5.24}$$

This can be compared with the actual value of the inverse of the matrix of second partials at the true minimum:

$$J (1, 1)^{-1} = \begin{bmatrix} .5 & 1 \\ 1 & 2.005 \end{bmatrix}$$

(5. 25)

A total of 287 function evaluations were required to complete the 22 iterations. This is an average of about 13 evaluations per iteration. Since 4 calculations always were required to estimate the two components of the gradient, this implies an average of about 9 evaluations per iteration required to find the minimum along the line to within the desired accuracy.

The value of $10^{-4}$ was found to be a good differencing interval for this problem only after comparing the results of several runs. For smaller choices of differencing interval it was found that the components of the calculated gradient had only two or three significant figures. This led to an erratic calculation of the new directions. Larger values of the differencing interval permitted higher-order derivatives in the expansion of the function to introduce serious errors into the estimate of the gradient. This occasionally caused the method to fail, when no lower point could be found to the side of the current point thought to be downhill. This possibility is illustrated in Fig. 5. 2.

For the Davidon method to work reliably one must find accurately the relative minimum in the iteration direction. However, one cannot choose the step size criterion number to be arbitrarily small. As smaller and smaller steps are taken, the divided difference formulas used in the parabolic interpolation suffer from the same truncation problem which limits the gradient. Hence, it is reasonable to choose the minimum-step criterion to be the same number as the gradient differencing interval.

5. 4    Two Design Examples

In Appendix A we discuss the Apollo spacecraft control problem. The problem has been separated into the design of an attitude control computer program and the design of a guidance steering-control program. A guidance law being considered as a possible steering program is a cross-product steer law:

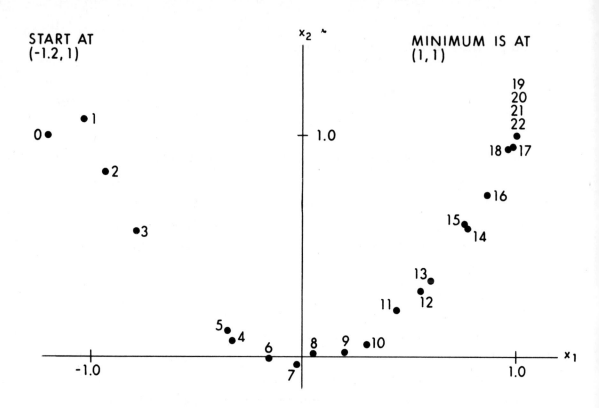

Fig. 5.1  Progress of the Method of Davidon when Used to Find the
Minimum of the Parabolic Valley

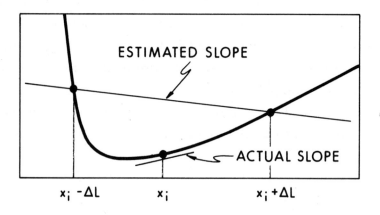

Fig. 5.2  The Sign of the Estimated Derivative May Disagree
with the Sign of the Actual Derivative

$$\Delta \underline{v}_i = \underline{v}_i - \underline{v}_{i-1}$$

(5.26)

$$\Delta \underline{\theta}c_i = K_i \frac{\Delta \underline{v}_i \times \underline{v}g_i}{|\Delta \underline{v}_i| \ |\underline{v}g_i|} \Delta t$$

The direction of the present acceleration is estimated from the back difference of readings from the integrating accelerometers. The calculated cross product is an estimate of the angle between the acceleration
and the velocity-to-be-gained. An increment to the commanded attitude
is sent to the attitude control autopilot. This increment is proportional
to the computed pointing error angle.

We evaluated the short burn performance of the cross-product
steering law in Section 2.6. For this evaluation we used a fifth-order
model to describe the plant, including center-of-mass offset, lateral
velocity, vehicle rotation rate, vehicle attitude, and the lag of the attitude control computer program. The quadratic cost formula which measured the quality of the design was

$$\text{cost} = \left[ \frac{1}{2} M \underline{v}^2 + \frac{1}{2} I \omega^2 \right]_{t=T} + \int_0^T w \, (\delta - \epsilon)^2 \, dt$$

(5.27)

This penalized the unwanted vehicle energy at cut-off due to lateral velocity and vehicle rotation rate  and also penalized the nozzle angle activity away from the angular location of the center-of-mass.

For a sampling interval of $\Delta t = 2$ sec. and a constant steering-
law gain of $K_i = .1$ we evaluated the performance of the design during
a 20-second burn. The results, summarized in Fig. 2.5, show a high-
velocity cut-off error of 7 ft/sec. RMS. The mean cost was found to
be 55,000 ft.-lb. of energy. (This includes both the terminal energy
and the integral square nozzle deviation, weighted with $w = 10^6$.)

In Section 4.2 we asked if there was room for improvement in
the design. With the Joseph and Tou synthesis for the optimal stochastic
controller we found that there was considerable room for improvement.
The optimal controller had a cut-off velocity error of only .08 ft/sec.
RMS. The mean cost was only 2600 ft.-lb. The performance of the

121

optimal steer law was shown in Fig. 4.1. Thus we are motivated to continue the design effort in search of a more effective practical design.

To gain some insight into the nature of an efficient steering program we can solve analytically a highly simplified optimization problem. We can replace the fifth-order dynamic description of the plant with a simple second-order model which retains only the unwanted lateral component of velocity $v_\perp$ and the vehicle attitude $\theta$ as state variables:

$$\dot{v}_\perp = a\theta$$
$$\dot{\theta} = \omega \tag{5.28}$$

The control variable here is considered to be the angular velocity $\omega$ of the vehicle. There is no noise driving the state and no noise in the measurement of velocity. Thus we can require as a terminal boundary condition that the unwanted component of velocity at cut-off be exactly zero. There are many ways to command $\omega$ to meet this terminal condition, but we will consider the optimum way to be the one which minimizes the cost given by

$$\text{cost} = \int_0^T \omega^2 \, dt \tag{5.29}$$

We consider the continuous control problem where the velocity is continuously monitored and the vehicle rate is continuously commanded.

This optimal control problem is easily solved using standard techniques from the calculus of variations. It can be shown that a necessary condition for $\omega(t)$ to be optimal is that it must be a linear function of time which reaches zero at cut-off $t = T$:

$$\omega_{opt} = c\,(T - t) \tag{5.30}$$

One then can solve for the choice of $c$ in terms of the given initial state $v_\perp(0)$, $\theta(0)$ and the duration of the operating period $T$. One thus finds the optimal open-loop control law:

$$\omega_{opt} = -\frac{3}{T} \left[ \frac{v_\perp(0)}{aT} + \theta(0) \right] \frac{(T - t)}{T} \tag{5.31}$$

But if we interpret $t = 0$ to be the present time and $T$ to be the time-to-go $T_{go}$, then one has the optimal closed-loop (feedback) control law:

122

$$\omega_{opt} = -\frac{3}{T_{go}}\left[\frac{v_\perp}{a\,T_{go}} + \theta\right] \tag{5.32}$$

We note that $-v_\perp/a\,T_{go}$ is the linearized expression for the inertial angle of the velocity-to-be-gained vector. Thus the quantity in brackets is the angle between the $v_g$ vector and the acceleration vector. It is just this angle which is estimated in the cross-product steering law. Thus an interesting result is that, for this simplified model, the optimal control law may be expressed as a cross-product steering law, provided the gain is time-varying as $3/T_{go}$:

$$\underline{\omega}_{cmd} = \frac{3}{T_{go}}\frac{a \times \underline{v}_g}{|\underline{a}|\,|\underline{v}_g|} \tag{5.33}$$

In this mathematically optimal controller, the steer-law gain goes to infinity as $T_{go}$ approaches zero. But the error angle between the acceleration and the velocity to-be-gained will go to zero faster, so that the resulting $\omega_{cmd}$ will decrease as required linearly to zero at cut-off.

Unfortunately in the actual control problem, where we have computer lags due to back differencing velocity and due to pulsing and holding the attitude command, a sampled-data approximation to the above control law would be unstable when approaching cut-off. This problem was encountered even with the constant gain steer law evaluated in Section 2.6. It was found necessary to suppress the change in attitude command for the last sample interval, to allow the vehicle angular velocity to stablize. The problem would be even more severe here if we allow the gain to go to infinity. A possible solution is to make use of the fact that in the simple problem under optimal control, the vehicle rotation rate should decrease linearly to zero at cut-off. If the estimated vehicle acceleration is about $\Delta t/2$ "old" because it is derived from a velocity back difference over $\Delta t$ sec., and if the attitude command of $\Delta\theta = \omega\Delta t$ appears to be too large because the average rotation rate actually desired over the next $\Delta t$ sec. is the rate appropriate for a time advanced by $\Delta t/2$ sec., then perhaps one can compensate for this total lag of about $\Delta t$ sec. by reducing the command linearly according to the relation of the effective lag and the time-to-go $T_{go}$. That is, we suggest a modified time-varying gain of

$$K = \frac{x_1}{T_{go}} \frac{(T_{go} - x_2)}{T_{go}} \tag{5.34}$$

where $x_1$ should be about 3 and $x_2$ should be about $\Delta t = 2$. For large $T_{go}$, the gain can match the continuous optimal value of $3/T_{go}$; but as cut-off approaches, the gain will go to zero. (We will not let the gain go negative, but will hold it at zero for $T_{go}$ less than $x_2$.)

A possible digital approximation to the suggested steer law would be

$$\Delta \underline{v}_i = \underline{v}_i - \underline{v}_{i-1}$$

$$T_{go_i} = \frac{|\underline{vg}_i|}{|\Delta \underline{v}_i|} \Delta t$$

$$K_i = \frac{x_1 (T_{go_i} - x_2)}{T_{go_i}^2} \tag{5.35}$$

$$\Delta \underline{\theta c}_i = K_i \frac{\Delta \underline{v}_i \times \underline{vg}_i}{|\Delta \underline{v}_i| \, |\underline{vg}_i|} \Delta t$$

This digital control computer program is not of significantly greater complexity than the constant gain cross-product steer law.

To determine the best values for the parameters $x_1$ and $x_2$ in the proposed time-varying control program, we consider the cost Eq. (5.27) to be a function only of $x_1$ and $x_2$. We can perform an automatic search for the values of $x_1$ and $x_2$ which will minimize the cost. We use the same five-dimensional model for the plant described in Section 2.6. We use the same linearized first-order state space representation Eq. (2.123) for the steering program, but with the new time-varying gain $K_i$. Program MINFINDER, incorporating the Davidon method as discussed in the previous section, is used to conduct the search for the best choice of the two free parameters. It calls a simple subroutine which provides the time-varying state space representation of the steering program as a function of the two parameters. This program in turn calls subroutine EVALUATOR which computes the mean cost of the current design. It is

124

thought that good values for the two parameters are $x_1 = 3$ and $x_2 = \Delta t = 2$, so these will be used for the starting point for the search. A good differencing interval for estimating the gradient was found to be $10^{-3}$. The criterion values for terminating each linear search and for terminating the entire run also was $10^{-3}$. A lower bound chosen for the minimum mean cost is 2631. This is the mean cost which would be achieved by the Joseph and Tou optimal stochastic controller if it could be realized at the same sample rate. We use the same cost weight $w = 10^6$ on the integral of the square of the nozzle angle away from the center-of-mass as was used to keep the nozzle activity in a reasonable range in the Joseph and Tou synthesis. The computer run made the following progress in searching for the minimum:

| iteration | mean cost | $x_1$ | $x_2$ | design evaluations |
|-----------|-----------|-------|-------|--------------------|
| 0 | 4125 | 3 | 2 | 1 |
| 1 | 3804 | 2.59 | 2.22 | 20 |
| 2 | 3753 | 2.75 | 2.63 | 33 |
| 3 | 3739.6 | 2.87 | 2.71 | 44 |
| 4 | 3738.66 | 2.907 | 2.778 | 55 |
| 5 | 3738.6588 | 2.9096 | 2.7806 | 63 |
| 6 | 3738.6587 | 2.9095 | 2.7803 | 70 |

It turns out that the original estimated values for the parameters of $x_1 = 3$ and $x_2 = 2$ perform quite well, with a cost of only 4125. The optimization of the simple design only changes the parameter values to $x_1 = 2.9$ and $x_2 = 2.8$, with a slight reduction of the cost to 3739. This optimized time-varying control program is quite an improvement over the constant-gain cross-product steer law evaluated in Section 2.6. The cut-off velocity error is only .21 ft/sec. RMS, the cut-off vehicle rotation rate is .24 degrees/sec., and the peak nozzle angle is 3.5 degrees. Like the optimal stochastic controller, whose performance was shown in Fig. 4.1, the peak nozzle angle occurs early in the operating period, rather than at the end. Since the performance of this time-varying steer law is close to the theoretical optimal performance of 2631, one

125

would be inclined to end the design effort — the point of diminishing returns having been reached.

As a check on the convergence of the search for the best choice of the two parameters, we reran the minimization program starting from different initial parameters $x_1 = 0$ and $x_2 = 0$. The computer run made the following progress in searching for the minimum:

| iteration | mean cost | $x_1$ | $x_2$ | design evaluations |
|---|---|---|---|---|
| 0 | 980, 055 | 0 | 0 | 1 |
| 1 | 5954 | 1. 70 | 0 | 17 |
| 2 | 5677 | 1. 70 | . 43 | 31 |
| 3 | 4410 | 2. 01 | 1. 72 | 46 |
| 4 | 4261 | 2. 07 | 1. 50 | 58 |
| 5 | 3783 | 2. 70 | 2. 67 | 73 |
| 6 | 3745 | 2. 79 | 2. 60 | 83 |
| 7 | 3738. 666 | 2. 9073 | 2. 7801 | 93 |
| 8 | 3738. 659 | 2. 9086 | 2. 7798 | 100 |

This second run converged to a similar design, in excellent agreement with the first run. The optimized parameters agree in value to an accuracy of the order of the given criterion number $10^{-3}$. The second run required more design evaluations to converge to the minimum cost design. This illustrates the obvious value of a good initial estimate for the design.

In Appendix B we review the air-to-air missile control problem, which was suggested by Johansen. We have used this problem to illustrate that in a computer-limited application a simplified control program by operating at a faster sampling rate can outperform a Joseph and Tou optimal stochastic controller. In Section 4. 2 we determined the minimum miss-distance that was possible under optimal control for various choices of sample interval $\Delta t$. The results were summarized in Fig. 4. 3. For a sufficiently small $\Delta t$ the miss-distance can be as small as 14 ft. RMS. We assumed that the available computer capacity was such that $\Delta t = .8$ would be required to realize a third-order Joseph and Tou

optimal stochastic control program. At such a sample interval the minimum miss-distance would be 31 ft. RMS. In Section 4.3 we designed a
second-order time-varying controller by synthesizing the Joseph and Tou
optimal controller for a simplified mathematical model for the problem.
This controller could operate at a sample interval of $\Delta t = .6$ sec., and
it had a miss-distance of 25 ft. RMS.

A first-order control computer program could operate with a
sample interval of $\Delta t = .4$ sec. Perhaps such a program could have even
better performance. As with the cross-product steering problem, we
shall solve a simplified version of the problem to suggest an efficient
design. The plant dynamics are simplified to include only

$$\dot{y} = v$$
$$\dot{v} = -a_m$$

(5.36)

where y is the lateral separation of the target and missile normal to the
initial line-of-sight, v is the lateral velocity, and $a_m$ is the lateral acceleration of the missile. We assume no target acceleration, no measurement noise and will use continuous control. It is possible to meet
perfectly the desired terminal condition of $y(T) = 0$. Many time-his-
tories $a_m(t)$ of missile acceleration can meet this terminal condition,
but we will consider the optimal one to be that which minimizes the cost
given by

$$cost = \int_0^T a_m^2 \, dt$$

(5.37)

This problem is mathematically identical to the second-order steering
problem solved earlier. We can write the solution to this problem by
inspection by taking the solution to the earlier problem Eq. (5.32) and
substituting y for $v_\perp / a$, v for $\theta$, and $-a_m$ for $\omega$. Thus we have the optimal missile acceleration given as

$$-a_m = -\frac{3}{T_{go}} \left[ \frac{y}{T_{go}} + v \right]$$

(5.38)

The measurement available is the inertial angle $\sigma$ of the line-of-sight
from the missile to the target. The state variable y may be derived
from the noise-free measurement as

127

$$y = v_c T_{go} \sigma \qquad (5.39)$$

where $v_c$ is the closing velocity. The time-derivating of Eq. (5.39) provides the state variable $v$ as

$$v = v_c T_{go} \dot{\sigma} - v_c \sigma \qquad (5.40)$$

Equations (5.39) and (5.40) can be used to reformulate the optimal missile acceleration in terms of the available measurement:

$$a_m = 3 v_c \dot{\sigma} \qquad (5.41)$$

This remarkably simple solution to the optimal control problem is well known and is called proportional navigation. Independent of the range, one should accelerate laterally proportional to the rate of change of the line-of-sight angle. The constant of proportionality should be three times the closing velocity.

A possible digital approximation to the indicated continuous control law could estimate the derivative from a back difference of the last two available measurements. Thus the computer program could be

$$a_{m_i} = \frac{3 v_c}{\Delta t} \sigma_i - \frac{3 v_c}{\Delta t} \sigma_{i-1} \qquad (5.42)$$

This result suggests that a first-order constant-coefficient control computer program might do quite well in the nonstationary third-order stochastic control problem. The most general first-order constant coefficient control program in canonical form may be written

$$a_{m_i} = s_i + x_1 \frac{v_c}{\Delta t} \sigma_i$$
$$\qquad (5.43)$$
$$s_{i+1} = x_3 s_i + x_2 \frac{v_c}{\Delta t} \sigma_i$$

where $x_1$, $x_2$, and $x_3$ are nondimensional constant coefficients and $s$ is the one computer state variable. Equation (5.42) is a special case of Eq. (5.43) where $x_1 = 3$, $x_2 = -3$, and $x_3 = 0$.

Again, we can perform an automatic search for the values of $x_1$, $x_2$, and $x_3$ which will minimize the cost. A good differencing interval

128

used to estimate the gradient was found to be $10^{-4}$. The criterion value for terminating each linear search and for terminating the entire run was also $10^{-4}$. A lower bound chosen for the minimum mean cost is 336. This is the mean cost achieved by the Joseph and Tou stochastic controller, optimal for the present sample interval of $\Delta t = .4$ sec. We use the same cost weight $w = 4.80 \times 10^{-4}$ on the integral of the square of the missile acceleration as was required to hold the peak acceleration of the Joseph and Tou synthesis to 400 ft/sec.$^2$ RMS. The initial trial values for the three free parameters are assumed to be $x_1 = 3$, $x_2 = -3$, and $x_3 = 0$. The computer run made the following progress in searching for the minimum cost design:

| iteration | mean cost | $x_1$ | $x_2$ | $x_3$ | design evaluations |
|-----------|-----------|-------|-------|-------|--------------------|
| 0 | 1024 | 3 | -3 | 0 | 1 |
| 1 | 834 | 2.80 | -3.01 | -.17 | 17 |
| 2 | 643 | 2.56 | -3.08 | -.20 | 37 |
| 3 | 553 | 2.21 | -2.23 | -.02 | 56 |
| 4 | 523.2 | 1.98 | -1.88 | .04 | 71 |
| 5 | 521.9 | 1.98 | -1.89 | .04 | 85 |
| 6 | 516.4 | 1.96 | -1.75 | .11 | 100 |
| 7 | 515.1 | 1.92 | -1.66 | .13 | 117 |
| 8 | 514.1 | 1.89 | -1.63 | .14 | 131 |
| 9 | 513.8 | 1.87 | -1.58 | .16 | 147 |

To conserve computer time, the run was stopped at 150 design evaluations. The run did not have sufficient time to converge, in the sense that the last step was to be less than $10^{-4}$. Nevertheless, the optimization procedure has cut the cost to half that of the initial trial design. The final cost of 514 compares quite favorably with the cost of 336 achieved by the Joseph and Tou third-order stochastic controller, optimal for this sample interval of $\Delta t = .4$ sec. The individual quantities of interest controlled by the optimized first-order design include a miss-distance of 19.8 ft. RMS and a peak missile acceleration of

325 ft/sec.$^2$ RMS occurring in the last control interval. The acceleration cost weight succeeded in holding the peak acceleration of the optimized design under 400 ft/sec.$^2$. With additional expenditure of computer time, one could refine the controller design by reducing the acceleration cost weight and then repeating the search. The resulting peak acceleration can be permitted to grow to 400 ft/sec.$^2$, and the resulting miss-distance would be smaller. In any case, we have shown that a remarkably simple constant-coefficient first-order control computer program can come quite close in performance to the optimal possible under time-varying third-order continuous control — 20 ft. RMS miss-distance as compared with 14 ft. RMS. And this simple control computer program outperforms the other realizable programs designed earlier.

These two design examples demonstrate that the optimization procedure for simplified controllers is a practical design method. At the outset one sets the complexity of the controller. But if the configuration is properly motivated, the resulting optimized design can realize good performance. In both of the design examples we used basically the same approach to motivate a simplified design structure: we solved analytically a simplified lower-order, continuous, noise-free problem. Other approaches would be equally valid and should also yield good results.

## 5.5    Other Promising Minimization Algorithms

A shortcoming of the computer program for minimization described in Section 5.3 was the method used to estimate the gradient. The method of differencing neighboring values of the function required that the user specify a size for the differencing interval. The interval must be sufficiently large to avoid floating point truncation problems, but sufficiently small so that the scale of the problem is not overstepped. Choice of the proper size is largely experimental, the results of several choices being compared to decide which choice is the most efficient. Thus some computer time is wasted in finding a good value for this parameter.

The problem could be avoided by using analytical formulas for the components of the gradient. One can derive a formula for the derivative of the cost with respect to a free parameter, which is similar in structure to the formula derived in Chapter 2 for the value of the cost.

130

It appears that the arithmetic required to evaluate one analytical derivative expression is roughly double the arithmetic required for one cost evaluation. It is an accident that the approximate method of forward-backward differencing, which we implemented in Section 5.3, requires two function evaluations for one derivative — hence also requires double the computer time of one cost evaluation. Thus the use of analytical gradient formulas would yield no improvement in the running time required by the Davidon method to converge to the minimum. Any savings would come from the elimination of experimental runs required to find a good differencing interval.

Alternate minimization techniques have been developed which do not require the calculation or estimation of derivatives. For example, Powell (1964) has developed a method which retains many of the features of the Davidon method, but which does not require derivatives. The method still requires searches for minima along lines, and after each iteration new directions are chosen so that rapid convergence is assured. Powell demonstrated his method with several test functions. It was able to find the minimum of Rosenbrock's parabolic valley with only 151 function evaluations. This is a good improvement over our application of Davidon's method, which required 287 function evaluations. In a review of methods for minimizing functions without evaluating derivatives, Fletcher (1965) points out some shortcomings of Powell's method; but he goes on to conclude that this method is the best available, in terms of number of function evaluations required to reach a minimum.

This conclusion is premature, because Fletcher did not test any methods based upon a Newton-Raphson iteration. We have programmed the Newton method, using differencing to to estimate not only the gradient but also the Jacobian. This program found the minimum of Rosenbrock's test function in only 135 function evaluations. The basic iterative step was discussed in Section 5.3 and is given by Eq. (5.5). To implement an iteration we estimated the gradient — as in the Davidon method — by differencing function values ahead and behind the current point. Then the diagonal entries of the Jacobian matrix can be estimated with no additional function evaluations. For example, the first element in a two-dimensional problem would be estimated from

$$J_{11} = \frac{1}{x_1^2} \left[ f(x_1, 0) - 2f(0, 0) + f(-x_1, 0) \right] \qquad (5.44)$$

The off-diagonal elements in the Jacobian matrix all require the evaluation of one additional point. In the two-dimensional example one must evaluate $f(x_1, x_2)$, and then the off-diagonal element would be computed as

$$J_{12} = \frac{1}{x_1 x_2} \left[ f(x_1, x_2) - f(x_1, 0) - f(0, x_2) + f(0, 0) \right] \qquad (5.45)$$

It can be shown that the error in these formulas is second-order with respect to the choice of differencing interval size $x_1$ and $x_2$. In an n-dimensional problem 2 n-function evaluations are required to estimate the gradient, and n (n - 1)/2 additional function evaluations are required to estimate the Jacobian.

In the minimization program, the step proposed by the Newton iteration Eq. (5.5) is attempted only if it is directed downhill. This test is based simply on the dot product of the indicated step with the estimated gradient. If the indicated step is uphill, then for that iteration the direction of steepest descent is used instead. The step size tried is based on Eq. (5.17), which locates the minimum of a parabola having the same value, slope, and minimum value. With either a Newton step or a steepest descent step, to guarantee stability a trial point is accepted as the new current point only if the trial is successful. If the trial step fails to produce a lower point, the step size is cut in half and the trial repeated.

A major difference between this application of the Newton method and the Davidon or Powell method is that each iteration terminates at the first success. There is no search along a line for a minimum. Thus a new direction is chosen more often. A major shortcoming of the Davidon or Powell method seems to be that these methods devote too much time refining the estimate of the location of the minimum along a line, rather than striking out in a new direction where more rapid improvement is possible.

While the result was excellent when applying the Newton minimization program to the Rosenbrock test function, the results were less successful when applying the program to the three-parameter

132

air-to-air missile design problem. Here, no good value for the differencing interval could be found, and progress toward the minimum was always slow.

A useful insight into the relative efficiency of programs which use derivatives as compared to programs which do not is provided by Jeeves (1958). Jeeves' result is also reported by Traub (1964). Jeeves compares the two best-known methods for solving the nonlinear scalar equation g (x) = 0. The first method is the Newton-Raphson iteration. Given the value of the function g and its derivative g' at the same point $x_1$, the next estimate $x_0$ of the location of the solution is given as

$$x_0 = x_1 - \frac{g(x_1)}{g'(x_1)} \tag{5.46}$$

The second method is the secant method, also called the method of false position (regula falsi) or the method of linear interpolation. Given the last two evaluations of the function, but no derivatives, the next estimate of the location of the solution is given as

$$x_0 = x_1 - g(x_1) \frac{x_2 - x_1}{g(x_2) - g(x_1)} \tag{5.47}$$

The Newton method is known to have a convergence factor of p = 2. That is, the increase in correct significant figures, in the estimate of the solution point x, is double the previous increase. The secant method is known to have a convergence factor somewhat less (p = $(1 + \sqrt{5})/2 \approx 1.6$). It terms of convergence per iteration the Newton method is superior. However, Jeeves points out that in terms of computer time required the secant method often is superior. This is because the secant method requires only one new function evaluation per iteration, whereas the Newton method requires not only one function evaluation but also one derivative evaluation per iteration. Jeeves derives a formula which gives the time required by the secant method relative to the time required by the Newton method, as a function of the time required to evaluate the derivative relative to the time required to evaluate the function:

133

$$T_{secant} = \frac{1.44}{1 + \dfrac{T_{derivative}}{T_{function}}} \; T_{newton} \qquad\qquad (5.48)$$

Thus he concludes that if evaluating the derivative requires more than 44% of the time required to evaluate the function, then the secant method is more efficient.

These ideas have been generalized to the problem of solving a system of nonlinear equations:

$$g_i (x_1, x_2, \ldots x_n) = 0 \qquad i = 1, 2, \ldots n \qquad\qquad (5.49)$$

We have already discussed the generalized Newton-Raphson iteration. If J is the Jacobian matrix, whose elements are

$$J_{ij} = \frac{\partial \, g_i}{\partial \, x_j} \qquad\qquad (5.50)$$

then the next estimate of the location of the solution is

$$\underline{x}_{i+1} = \underline{x}_i - J(\underline{x}_i)^{-1} \, \underline{g}(\underline{x}_i) \qquad\qquad (5.51)$$

Wolfe (1959) has developed a generalization of the secant method. The method does not require the explicit evaluation of the matrix J, but rather works with the last n+1 evaluations of $\underline{g}$, where n is the number of variables. Each iteration requires only a new evaluation of $\underline{g}$. Barnes (1965) discusses the relative rate of convergence of the generalized Newton method compared with the generalized secant method. For the purpose of comparison he assumed the matrix J would have to be estimated numerically by differencing n+1 neighboring evaluations of $\underline{g}$, so each Newton-Raphson iteration was scored as n+1 evaluations of $\underline{g}$. With this assumption, he derived the ratio r of the number of g evaluations required by the Newton method to the number of g evaluations required by the secant method (in order to achieve the same accuracy) as a function of the number of variables n.

| n | 1 | 2 | 3 | 4 | . . . | 10 | . . . | 100 |
|---|---|---|---|---|-------|----|-------|-----|
| r | 1.39 | 1.65 | 1.86 | 2.03 | . . . | 2.68 | . . . | 4.91 |

He concluded that in problems where the Jacobian must be estimated numerically, and especially in problems of high dimension, the secant method is superior.

The method of Wolfe and Barnes can be applied to the problem of function minimization. Searching for the minimum of the function f (x) is the same as looking for the point where the gradient g (x) of the function is zero. The Newton method is not so unfavorable in the minimization problem, because here the Jacobian is symmetric:

$$J_{ij} = \frac{\partial}{\partial x_j} (g_i) = \frac{\partial}{\partial x_j} \left( \frac{\partial f}{\partial x_i} \right) = \frac{\partial}{\partial x_i} \left( \frac{\partial f}{\partial x_j} \right) = \frac{\partial}{\partial x_i} (g_j) = J_{ji} \qquad (5.52)$$

Hence only half the off-diagonal entries need be evaluated. In the program implementing the Newton method, which we discussed earlier, 2 n-evaluations of f were required to estimate g and n (n - 1)/2 additional evaluations of f were required to estimate J. Thus the number of function evaluations required for one Newton iteration compared with the number of function evaluations required for one secant iteration is

$$\frac{2n + \dfrac{n (n - 1)}{2}}{2 n} = 1 + \frac{n - 1}{4} \qquad (5.53)$$

This ratio is always smaller than n+ 1, which is the relative cost assumed by Barnes in his study. Thus it may turn out that some variant of the Newton method is better for low-order problems.

As the computational techniques for finding the minimum of a function become more advanced, the method for optimizing simplified controller designs will become even more attractive.

# Chapter 6

## Conclusion

### 6.1 Summary of Results

The increasing use of digital computers to control continuous processes requires more systematic procedures for the design of the control
computer programs. We have considered the design of optimal time-varying controllers for processes having random disturbances. We limited
our attention to linear controllers and linear plants. We further assumed
that the control objectives could be stated adequately by a quadratic cost
functional.

With a linear controller operating a linear plant in a stochastic
environment, it is not necessary to run several simulations of the system in order to evaluate the average performance of the controller. It
is possible to use an explicit evaluation technique where the RMS values
of all the quantities of interest are calculated as a function of time. The
overall mean quadratic operating cost also is calculated explicitly.

Joseph and Tou provided a direct synthesis procedure for finding a sampled-data controller which will minimize the mean value of
the cost. One should cascade a Kalman estimator of the plant state
variables with a Kalman-Koepcke deterministic controller. We pointed
out that the Joseph and Tou controller does not have a unique structure.
One may transform the state space of the indicated control computer
program without necessarily altering the transmission of the control
program from measurements to control signals. This freedom may be
exploited to minimize the arithmetic required of the control computer.
We developed two canonical forms for the controller which both require
$m^2$ less gains than the maximum (m is the dimension of the state space).
It is hoped that by reducing the required arithmetic, trial control programs
designed by optimal control theory may be used in more computer-limited
applications than would otherwise be possible.

137

A sampled-data system will not be able to control a plant as tightly as a controller which continuously absorbs information about the process and continuously modifies the control signals. This point has not been emphasized adequately in the literature of optimal sampled-data controllers. Where the capacity of the control computer is limited, a simplified control computer program by operating with a short sample interval may outperform the Joseph and Tou optimal controller operating with a longer sample interval. The Joseph and Tou controller is optimal only in the sense that no other controller at the same sample interval can outperform it.

There are many indirect ways that the algorithms of the Joseph and Tou synthesis can be used to assist the designer in a computer-limited application. Through several examples we attempted to illustrate some possible applications. Perhaps the most valuable contribution of optimal control theory is to provide a standard against which practical designs can be measured. Synthesizing and evaluating the optimal controller enables the design engineer to determine quickly whether or not his conflicting design objectives simultaneously can be met. Stated another way, the optimal controller demonstrates the theoretical limits of performance imposed on any design by imperfect information about the state of the plant, by disturbances driving the plant, by constraints on the control levels, and by the natural dynamics of the plant.

In other applications we demonstrated how the algorithms for the synthesis of optimal controllers might be used to suggest simplified designs. If the design engineer will make intelligent judgments as to how the mathematical model of the stochastic process can be simplified while retaining the essential aspects of the problem, then the optimal time-varying controller for the simplified model may be a practical design for controlling the actual process. This is a trial-and-error procedure which cannot eliminate the need for the knowledge of the experienced designer. But it does retain some of the advantages of optimal synthesis: Having formulated a mathematical model for the process and having specified the design objectives in an analytical cost formula, the trial design can be produced automatically by a digital computer, with no tedious labor required of the engineer. Thus one can explore various mathematical models and cost statements, evaluating the resulting designs, until a simple effective controller is found.

Constant-coefficient sampled-data controllers can be optimal in stationary regulator applications. Franklin and later Chang developed procedures for finding the optimal sampled-data regulator using spectral factorization techniques. An alternate way of producing such an optimal design is to use the Joseph and Tou synthesis procedure. Over a sufficiently long operating period in a stationary application, the resulting design will have constant coefficients for a period sufficiently far from both the initial time and the terminal time. The time-domain synthesis procedure is better suited to machine computation than the frequency domain procedure. Special treatment is not required for non-minimum phase plants or unstable plants or for multi-input multi-output systems. By means of these techniques we designed a fifth-order controller for the attitude of a flexible spacecraft.

For optimizing simplified controller designs we have applied the design philosophy of Phillips to time-varying sampled-data controllers. We discussed briefly the problem of finding a trial controller structure likely to permit good performance. The designer may leave several parameters in the design free for optimization. The computation of the mean operating cost of a trial design defines the cost as a function of the free parameters. We demonstrated that the method of Davidon was an effective numerical procedure for finding the minimum-cost optimized design. This design procedure is very practical. At the outset the design complexity is fixed at a reasonable level. Then within the complexity constraint the best design can be found.

The intent of this work has been to exploit and further develop a number of approaches to the utilization of optimal estimation and control theory and of modern digital computers in designing and evaluating practical feedback control systems. Examples have been given to illustrate the suggested techniques and to demonstrate the success of the approaches.

## 6.2   Suggestions for Further Study

In exploring design techniques for producing nearly optimal controllers we made some assumptions which are not always valid. One important assumption has been that the coefficients of the linear differential equations governing the plant are known. The optimality of the Joseph and Tou synthesis depends on this assumption. We pointed out that the "optimal" program to control the attitude of the flexible spacecraft, which we synthesized in Section 4.4, is highly tuned to the supposedly known frequency of the vehicle bending mode. If the bending frequency is not as anticipated, the closed-loop design might be unstable. Therefore an important problem is the design of optimal controllers where the plant characteristics are uncertain. The uncertain parameters may be treated as additional state variables to be estimated. Unfortunately this becomes a nonlinear estimation problem because one now has products of state variables in the dynamic description of the plant. To design optimal nonlinear estimators is a difficult problem. Fisher (1966) has shown that in general the optimal nonlinear estimator needs the exact conditional probability distribution of the state given the noisy measurements. In terms of statistical moments, this implies that one needs not only the mean and variance of all distributions but also an infinite sequence of the higher moments. Thus one is faced with an approximation problem. How much of the higher statistical information can be collected in a practical problem? What will be the errors if higher moments are assumed to be zero? One approximation technique has been suggested by Ho and Lee (1964). The nonlinear state space description perhaps can be linearized around nominal values for the state variables. Then the optimal linear estimator is designed for the linearized system. The separation theorem of Joseph and Tou probably is no longer valid with a nonlinear process. So even if one can master the nonlinear estimation problem, it may be that one is still a long way from having a systematic procedure for synthesizing optimal stochastic controllers for plants with uncertain parameters.

For convenience, we assumed that an efficient design could be synthesized by finding an appropriate weighting to be placed on the integral of the square of the control variables. That is, where the control effort had to be constrained below reasonable peak levels, we used a simple integral square penalty to constrain the peak RMS value. We recognized that the resulting design might not be truly optimal, because an alternate design utilizing maximum control over a longer interval might better reduce the unwanted deviations of other quantities of interest. An area for further study therefore is concerned with control variable constraints. One can conceive of an iterative procedure whereby one searches for a time-varying weighting on the square of the control variable which leads to a design everywhere utilizing the maximum permissible RMS control. Can an _explicit_ procedure be found for designing stochastic controllers with RMS limits on the control variables?

Limiting the peak RMS control value is a reasonable design objective where the tolerable limit is "soft." For example, the specified permissible missile acceleration can be set sufficiently low so that 99% of all flights will not exceed the structural limits of the missile. A more difficult problem is the design of efficient controllers where there are "hard" limits on the control variable. In these applications one really needs a design theory based on the admissible range of the control signals. The optimal controller necessarily will be nonlinear. One attempt at solving this problem is given by Sworder (1966). He considers the special case where all state variables are directly measurable by the feedback controller. He is able to obtain a theoretical solution to the problem, but much of the analytical simplification usually associated with linear system quadratic cost problems is lost. The computation of the solution to a very simple first-order problem was quite involved. It is not clear whether this approach will succeed with problems of practical order.

A different approach to the problem perhaps can evolve from the theory of minimum settling-time controllers. Several authors, including Pontryagin (1962) and Athans (1966), have shown that when all the state variables of the linear plant are accessible to the controller and when there are no plant disturbances, the minimum settling-time controller is a relay type controller — always utilizing the full control effort available. The optimal switching law is a nonlinear memoryless function of the plant state. To what extent can this theory for deterministic plants with bounded controls be extended to the stochastic control problem?

Further work should be directed toward methods for suggesting efficient trial controller designs. The design philosophy of Phillips requires that one first make an intelligent guess as to a controller structure likely to yield good performance. We pointed out that one procedure for developing a trial design is to first solve a simpler problem. Another example of this procedure for suggesting lower-order designs could be based on the work of Deyst (1964) and Bryson (1965). They pointed out that if some components of the measurement are perfect (not corrupted by uncorrelated noise), then the order of the optimal estimator is reduced. Perhaps one could set small measurement noises to zero, could synthesize the lower-order estimator, and could thus develop a lower-order controller which would operate well in the stochastic environment.

The order of the optimal stochastic controller may again be lower than the order of the plant if there is no penalty on the control. For example, suppose one wishes to design the optimal regulator for the simple first-order plant whose state x is the integral of the control u plus noise n and whose state can be observed by a noisy measurement y:

$$\dot{x} = u + n$$
$$y = x + w$$

(6.1)

It can be shown that the optimal sampled-data stochastic controller would have a z-transform given by

$$\frac{U}{Y}(z) = -ck\frac{[z + (1 - c\,\Delta t)\,(1 - k)]}{[z - (1 - c\,\Delta t)\,(1 - k)]}$$

(6.2)

where k is the optimal estimator gain related to the plant disturbance and the measurement noise, and c is the optimal deterministic controller gain related to the penalty weight placed on the state and the penalty weight placed on the control. In general the optimal controller is first order, matching the order of the plant. But if the measurement noise is zero, the optimal estimator gain is k = 1, the pole and zero of the optimal compensation cancel, and the resulting optimal controller is zero-order:

$$u_i = -c\,y_i$$

(6.3)

Similarly, if there is no penalty on control, the optimal controller gain is $c\,\Delta t = 1$, the pole and zero of the optimal compensation cancel, and the resulting optimal stochastic controller is zero order:

$$u_i\,\Delta t = -k\,y_i$$

(6.4)

Perhaps, in analogy with zero measurement noise theory, one can develop a zero control penalty theory, and this theory would be of use in suggesting simplified controller designs.

In addition to identifying the theoretical situations under which the optimal stochastic controller may be of lower order than the plant, it would be desirable to have a numerical procedure for automatically reducing the order of the controller. Kalman (1963) has discussed the relationship of state space representations to input-output (transfer function) representations. Transfer functions are related only to the part of the system which is both controllable and observable. Kalman discusses ways of finding that part of a state space representation which is both controllable and observable. This suggests a possible design procedure: One might synthesize the optimal stochastic controller according to the theory of Joseph and Tou. The order will match that of the plant. Now with a numerical procedure related to Kalman's ideas, transform the state-space representation so as to identify those modes which are strongly both controllable and observable. It is not necessary to use theoretical knowledge of why some modes are not controlled or observed (such as small measurement noise or small control weight). Having found any such modes, they may be discarded, with a resulting reduction of the order of the controller. It is not clear whether these ideas can be adapted to time-varying systems.

We discussed the optimization of controller designs by varying free parameters to minimize the cost. We applied the Davidon minimization technique to this problem and demonstrated that it can yield useful results. The improvement of the current tools available for the numerical minimization of a function was considered beyond the scope of this work. Nevertheless, it is an important area for future research, because the efficiency of the minimization tools directly determines the extent to which more ambitious design problems can be attacked. The generalized Newton method or the Wolfe-Barnes generalization of the secant method are promising minimization algorithms. It may turn out that the secant method is more reliable. We mentioned that we had difficulty finding a satisfactory differencing interval for the Newton method. No such difficulty arose with the Davidon method. Perhaps this is because in the Davidon method the quadratic information is inferred from widely spaced gradient information. If this is true, then the Wolfe-Barnes secant method would have the same advantage.

Yet to be developed is a descent method where each new function evaluation is carried out at the estimated location of the minimum, based on the previous function evaluations. No evaluations should be required in a small region to estimate either the Jacobian or the gradient. Rather, each additional point should be an attempt to reach the minimum. Estimates of the gradient and Jacobian, which are required for rapid convergence, would be developed implicitly.

These areas suggested for further study have been selected, not because progress may come easily, but rather because of their great importance in practical design problems.

# APPENDIX A

## The Apollo Spacecraft Control Problem

Several interesting problems involving computer control of a continuous plant can be found in the Apollo project. One configuration of the Apollo spacecraft includes the command and service module with the lunar excursion module docked (see Fig. A.1). This configuration is used during the portions of the mission after leaving earth orbit and until completion of deboost into lunar orbit. During this period, the main engine of the service module must be ignited to perform mid-course corrections to the trajectory of the spacecraft. For these short burn corrections, the vehicle is aligned initially in the right direction by maneuvering the vehicle with the small attitude control jets. During the burn, the proper heading is maintained by gimballing the large thrusting engine. The control function must be performed automatically by the onboard guidance computer. The computer receives information on the state of the vehicle through the inertial measurement unit. The measurements available are the inertial attitude (from gimbal angles of the gyro stabilized platform) and the velocity change produced by thrusting (from integrating accelerometers mounted on the platform). Using the measured attitude and velocity, the computer must send out nozzle angle commands in order to stabilize the flexible vehicle and to steer to the desired cut-off conditions.

A detailed mathematical description of this control problem can be very complex. We will consider the control problem in the pitch plane only. We will include the dynamics of the most significant bending mode (bending at the docking tunnel joining the LEM to the command module). We will neglect the higher-frequency bending modes and the dynamics of fuel slosh. We will assume that the short burn guidance objective is to acquire a certain velocity increment (without a constraint on position). We assume that this required velocity increment $v_r$ defined at the beginning of the burn is not a function of time or position. It does not rotate in inertial space. This is a reasonable approximation for short duration burns. Some of the velocity vectors defined in this problem are illustrated in Chapter 2, Fig. 2.3. Consistent with these assumptions a linearized mathematical model for the control process is a seventh-order state space representation. The fundamental differential equations governing the state variables are

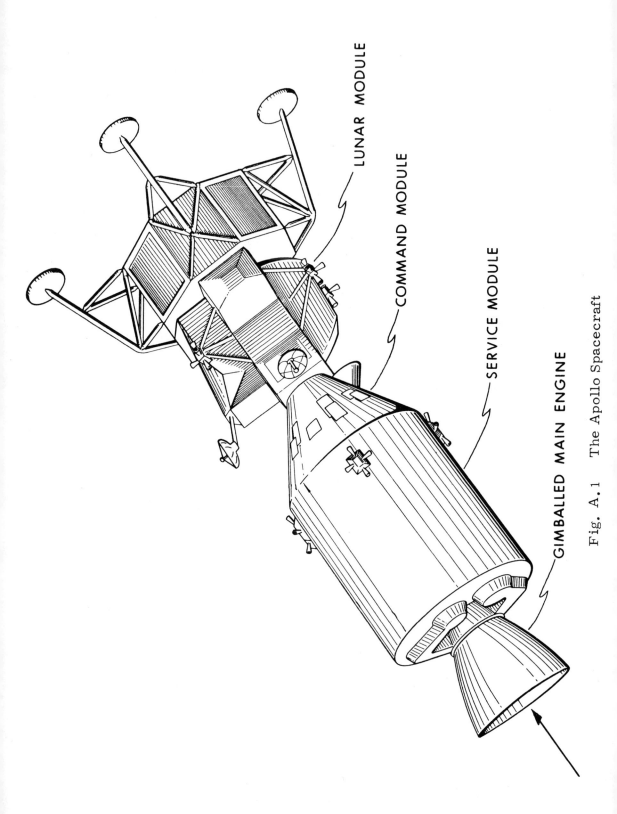

LUNAR MODULE

COMMAND MODULE

SERVICE MODULE

GIMBALLED MAIN ENGINE

Fig. A.1   The Apollo Spacecraft

146

$$\frac{d}{dt} \epsilon = 0 \tag{A.1}$$

$$\frac{d}{dt} v_\perp = a \theta(t) + a \sigma_T q(t) - a(\delta(t) + n(t)) \tag{A.2}$$

$$\frac{d}{dt} \omega = -\frac{TL}{I} \epsilon(t) - \frac{T}{I}(L \sigma_T + d_T) q(t) + \frac{TL}{I}(\delta(t) + n(t)) \tag{A.3}$$

$$\frac{d}{dt} \theta = \omega(t) \tag{A.4}$$

$$\frac{d}{dt} v_b = a d_T \epsilon(t) - \omega_b^2 q(t) - a d_T(\delta(t) + n(t)) \tag{A.5}$$

$$\frac{d}{dt} q = v_b(t) \tag{A.6}$$

$$\frac{d}{dt} \delta = -\frac{1}{\tau} \delta(t) + \frac{1}{\tau} \delta_c \tag{A.7}$$

The measurements available are

$$v_a = v_\perp(t) + L_a \omega(t) + d_a v_b(t) + w_v(t) \tag{A.8}$$

$$\theta_a = \theta(t) + \sigma_a q(t) + w_\theta(t) \tag{A.9}$$

The physical meaning of each of the seven state variables is:

$\epsilon$      The angular offset of the center-of-mass of the unbent vehicle (angle away from the centerline as seen from the engine gimbal station). The significance of this unknown angle is that the thrust vector initially is not aligned through the center-of-mass. The vehicle therefore will turn off course.

$v_\perp$      The unwanted component of velocity of the center-of-mass of the vehicle. This component is perpendicular to the initial required velocity increment, which defines the inertial reference direction for the short burn.

ω      The angular velocity of the underlying rigid vehicle.

$\theta$      The inertial attitude of the underlying rigid vehicle, relative to the inertial reference direction.

$v_b$      The velocity of the generalized bending coordinate.

q      The generalized bending coordinate.

$\delta$      The angle of the nozzle of the main engine relative to centerline of the bottom end of the service module.

In addition to the state variables we have defined two measurements and several disturbance variables:

$v_a$      The measured velocity at the inertial-measurement-unit station. This includes center-of-mass motion, plus motion of the station relative to the center-of-mass, plus measurement noise.

$\theta_a$      The measured attitude at the inertial-measurement-unit station, including bending effects and measurement noise.

$w_v$      The noise in the velocity measurements.

$w_\theta$      The noise in the attitude measurements.

n      A white noise vibrational disturbance at the bottom end of the service module, due to the rocket engine. We assume this disturbance enters the system of equations as a white noise random thrust vector angle.

In studying short burn designs, we assume that all of the coefficients in the above equations are constant. The assumed values for each of the parameters are

$a = 10$ ft./sec.$^2$      The magnitude of the acceleration of the vehicle due to thrusting.

T = 22000 pounds     The thrusting force of the engine.

M = 2200 slugs       The mass of the vehicle.

L = 19 ft.           The distance that the vehicle center-of-mass lies ahead of the engine.

$L_a$ = 0 ft.        The distance that the inertial-measurement-unit lies ahead of the vehicle center-of-mass.

I = 370000 slug ft.$^2$   The pitch moment-of-inertia of the rigid vehicle.

$\omega_b$ = 10 radians/sec.   The natural frequency of the bending mode.

$d_T$ = 1.1 ft./ft.   The displacement of the bending mode at the engine station (per unit displacement of the generalized coordinate).

$d_a$ = -1.3 ft./ft.   The displacement of the bending mode at the inertial-measurement-unit station (per unit displacement of the generalized coordinate).

$\sigma_T$ = -.13 radian/ft.   The slope of the bending mode at the engine station (per unit displacement of the generalized coordinate).

$\sigma_a$ = -.13 radian/ft.   The slope of the bending mode at the inertial-measurement-unit station (per unit displacement of the generalized coordinate).

$\tau$ = .1 sec.   The first-order lag with which the nozzle angle follows the commanded nozzle angle.

For a development of the normal mode description of structural bending, the reader is referred to Bisplinghoff, Ashley, and Halfman (1955).

A source of noise in the measurements is related to the quantization size of the analogue-to-digital conversion. If we assume that the quantization error is uniformly distributed over one quantization interval Q, then the statistics of the measurement error include

$$\text{mean error} = 0 \qquad\qquad (A.10)$$

$$\text{mean-squared error} = \frac{1}{12} Q^2 \tag{A.11}$$

The sizes of the velocity and attitude quantization are

$$Q_V = .2 \text{ ft./sec.}$$

$$Q_\theta = .0002 \text{ radians}$$

We will assume that the measurement error due to quantization is uncorrelated from measurement to measurement. This is a good approximation when the state variables are changing rapidly, but it is a bad approximation if the state variables are static.

The white noise random thrust vector angle n is assumed to have a low-frequency spectral density of

$$N = .0004 \text{ radians}^2 \text{ per cycle-per-second}$$

For a physical interpretation of the strength of this disturbance, consider an approximation to Eq. (A.2)

$$\frac{d}{dt} v_\perp = - a\, n(t) \tag{A.12}$$

The solution to this equation may be written

$$v_\perp(t) = - a \int_0^t n(\tau)\, d\tau \tag{A.13}$$

The mean-squared value of the lateral velocity is therefore

$$E\, v_\perp^2(t) = a^2 \int_0^t \int_0^t E\, n(\tau_1)\, n(\tau_2)\, d\tau_1\, d\tau_2 \tag{A.14}$$

The expectation in the integrand is the autocorrelation of the white noise, which is equal to N times the Dirac delta function $\delta(\tau_1 - \tau_2)$. Thus the integral can be evaluated explicitly, and the mean-squared value of the lateral velocity is

$$E v_\perp^2 (t) = a^2 N t \qquad (A. 15)$$

Considering the assumed value for vehicle acceleration (a = 10 ft/sec.$^2$) and the assumed density of the noise (N = .0004 rad$^2$/cps), Eq. (A. 15) shows that in the first second the noise causes a root-mean-square lateral velocity of one quantum (.2 ft/sec). Or in 100 seconds the noise has caused a lateral velocity of 10 quanta (2 ft/sec).

The initial statistics assumed for the vehicle state at the beginning of the burn include nonzero values for the center-of-mass offset angle $\epsilon$ and the initial inertial attitude $\theta$. The unknown component of the angular location of the center-of-mass is assumed to have

mean value $\epsilon$ = 0

RMS $\epsilon$ = .02 radians (about 1 degree)

The initial pointing error of the vehicle is assumed to have

mean value $\theta$ = 0

RMS $\theta$ = .01 radian (about $\frac{1}{2}$ degree)

All other components of the state are assumed to be initially zero. That is, the lateral velocity is (by definition) zero, the angular velocity of the vehicle is zero, the bending coordinate and velocity are both zero, and the nozzle is centered at zero angle.

For the control problem outlined above one must design a computer control program which takes two inputs (velocity and attitude) and sends out one output (commanded nozzle angle). In a practical solution to this design problem, the functions of the computer have been separated into two parts (See Fig. A. 2). The two-input single-output design problem is replaced by two single-input single-output design problems. First an attitude control loop is designed to operate only on the attitude error information. This is a high sample rate loop which is intended to stabilize the modes of the vehicle. Then secondly a steering loop is designed to operate only on the velocity information. This is a low sample rate loop which is

151

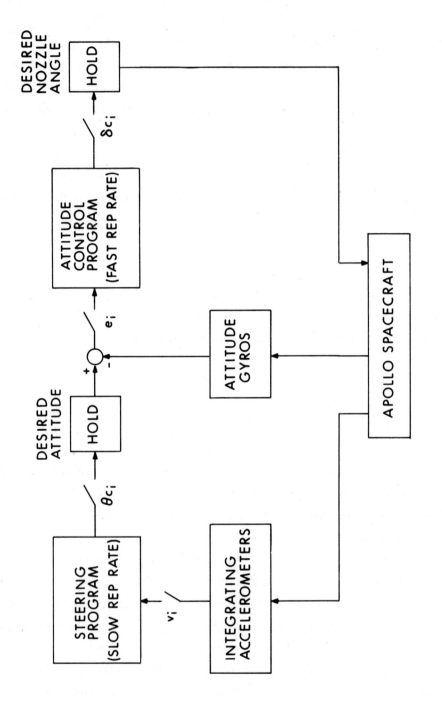

Fig. A.2   The Separation of Steering and Control in the Apollo Guidance Computer

supposed to change the commanded attitude so as to steer the vehicle to the desired cut-off conditions.

When considering the design of the steering program only, the plant is considered to include not only the vehicle but also the digital attitude control computer program. One proposed design for the attitude control program is presented by Stubbs (1965). In our studies of the steering program design, we will approximate this attitude control program with a simple continuous lead-lag filter, having the same low-frequency gain and phase characteristics. We will neglect the nozzle actuator lag as being fast compared with the lag in the attitude control program. Thus the nozzle angle $\delta$ is related to the attitude error by the transfer function

$$\frac{\delta}{\theta_c - \theta} = k \frac{s + \omega_z}{s + \omega_p} \qquad (A.16)$$

Since (in this mathematical model) step discontinuities in the control signal $\theta_c$ cause step discontinuties in the nozzle angle $\delta$, we cannot choose $\delta$ as a state variable. But if we remove the high-pass part of Eq. (A.16), there does remain a true state variable r. A state representation of Eq. (A.16) is then

$$\delta = k(\theta_c - \theta) + r \qquad (A.17)$$

$$\frac{d}{dt} r = -\omega_p r - k(\omega_p - \omega_z)(\theta_c - \theta) \qquad (A.18)$$

The parameter values required to match the low-frequency characteristics of the design by Stubbs are

$$k = 1.2$$

$$\omega_z = .2 \text{ radians /sec.}$$

$$\omega_p = 2 \text{ radians / sec.}$$

We can use Eq. (A.17) to eliminate the nozzle angle $\delta$ from the vehicle state equations, Eqs. (A.2) and (A.3). We ignore the bending mode, Eqs. (A.5) and (A.6). We assume the vibrational noise n(t) is zero. Then for steering

153

program design studies we have a simplified fifth-order model for the plant, which relates the commanded attitude $\theta_c$ to the resulting measurement of velocity $v_a$

$$\frac{d}{dt} \epsilon = 0 \tag{A.19}$$

$$\frac{d}{dt} v_\perp = a(1+k)\,\theta(t) - a\,r(t) - a\,k\,\theta_c \tag{A.20}$$

$$\frac{d}{dt} \omega = -\frac{TL}{I}\epsilon(t) - \frac{TL}{I}k\,\theta(t) + \frac{TL}{I}r(t) + \frac{TL}{I}k\,\theta_c \tag{A.21}$$

$$\frac{d}{dt} \theta = \omega(t) \tag{A.22}$$

$$\frac{d}{dt} r = (\omega_p - \omega_z)k\,\theta(t) - \omega_p r(t) - (\omega_p - \omega_z)k\,\theta_c \tag{A.23}$$

$$v_a = v_\perp(t) + L_a\,\omega(t) + w_v(t) \tag{A.24}$$

# APPENDIX B

## An Air-to-Air Missile Control Problem

An interesting third-order control problem appears in the thesis by Johansen (1964). An air-to-air missile is launched at a target. The launch direction is along the initial line-of-sight to the target. The target performs random evasive maneuvers. The missile has an inertially stabilized tracking radar, with which it can measure the angular location of the target with respect to the initial line-of-sight. The guidance system (to be designed) must process the noisy measurements of the target angular location and decide how to steer the missile so as to intercept the target. The control variable is considered to be the missile lateral acceleration. It is assumed that an autopilot is instrumented to produce actual missile accelerations which match the accelerations commanded by the guidance. Any lag in this closed-loop autopilot is assumed short compared with the dynamics of the guidance problem and is therefore neglected. The engine of the missile acts as a velocity sustainer. We assume that the closing velocity between the missile and the target is essentially constant. In evaluating the performance of any proposed guidance system we will be looking for the smallest possible miss-distance that can be achieved, consistent with missile accelerations being held below a reasonable level. Johansen explored continuous controllers. We, on the other hand, will assume that the missile has a small digital computer on board, and we will explore the design of efficient control computer programs employing sampled data.

The interception problem is illustrated in Fig. B. 1. We will use the linearized pitch-plane-only mathematical description suggested by Johansen. The state variables of the problem are considered to be: the relative lateral distance y between the target and the missile (measured normal to the initial line-of-sight), the relative lateral velocity v between the target and the missile, and the lateral acceleration $a_t$ of the target alone. The control variable is the lateral acceleration of the missile $a_m$. The fundamental differential equations governing the state variables are

$$\frac{d}{dt} y = v(t) \tag{B.1}$$

$$\frac{d}{dt} v = a_t(t) - a_m \tag{B.2}$$

155

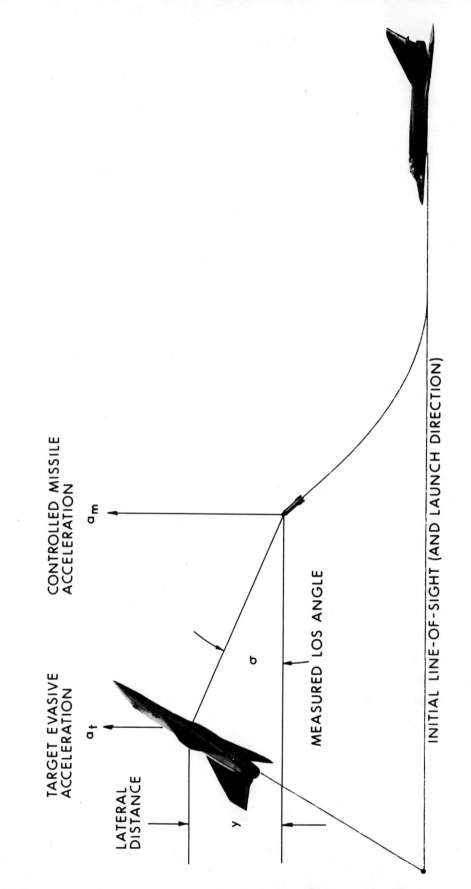

CONTROLLED MISSILE ACCELERATION

$a_m$

TARGET EVASIVE ACCELERATION

$a_t$

LATERAL DISTANCE

$y$

MEASURED LOS ANGLE

$\sigma$

INITIAL LINE-OF-SIGHT (AND LAUNCH DIRECTION)

Fig. B.1   The Air-to-Air Missile Intercepting a Target

$$\frac{d}{dt} a_t = -\frac{1}{\tau} a_t(t) + n(t) \tag{B.3}$$

where $n(t)$ is a white noise. One selects the appropriate level for the power density $N$ of the white noise based upon knowledge of the RMS target acceleration $\beta$ and the correlation time $\tau$ of the target acceleration:

$$N = \frac{2\beta^2}{\tau} \tag{B.4}$$

The measurement of the line-of-sight angle $\sigma$ is described by

$$\sigma(t) = \frac{1}{v_c t_{go}} y(t) + w(t) \tag{B.5}$$

where $v_c$ is the closing velocity, $t_{go}$ is the time-to-go until interception, and $w(t)$ is a short correlation-time random measurement error. The mean-square value $W$ of the measurement error is assumed known to be

$$W_i = \frac{1}{\Delta t} \left( \frac{r_1}{v_c^2 t_{go_i}^2} + r_2 \right) \tag{B.6}$$

The first term is related to the size of the target. Its importance grows as the target subtends a larger angle. The second term is related to the angular resolution of the radar and is not time dependent. The mean-square value of the measurement noise is shown inversely proportional to the choice of computer sampling interval. This could imply that the response time of the tracking radar is designed to match the computer sampling interval. For a short $\Delta t$ and therefore a fast radar, there is less integration time to smooth the measurement, and hence there is a larger measurement error in a sample. (Also the assumed dependence of the noise level upon $\Delta t$ yields the same low-frequency power density as the white measurement noise assumed by Johansen in his continuous design problem.)

The statistics of the initial state at launch are as follows: The initial lateral displacement $y$ between the target and the missile is by definition zero. Thus the mean value of $y(0)$ and the mean-square value of $y(0)$ are both zero. The initial lateral velocity difference between the target and the missile is assumed to have zero mean but a nonzero mean-square value. The initial target acceleration is assumed to have zero mean and mean-square value consistent with the stationary mean-square acceleration already discussed.

The numerical values assumed for each of the parameters in the problem are

$T$ = 12 sec.                    The duration of the flight from launch to interception.

$v_c$ = 3000 ft/sec.            The closing velocity.

$\beta$ = 32.2 ft/sec.$^2$      RMS target acceleration.

$\tau$ = 2.5 sec.               Correlation time of the target acceleration.

$r_1$ = 15 ft.$^2$ - sec.       Target size-related measurement noise.

$r_2$ = 1.5 × 10$^{-5}$ rad.$^2$ - sec.    Radar angular resolution measurement noise.

RMS $y$ (0) = 0 ft.             Root-mean-square initial lateral distance.

RMS $v$ (0) = 200 ft/sec.       Root-mean-square initial lateral velocity

RMS $a_t$(0) = $\beta$ ft/sec.$^2$    Root-mean-square initial target lateral acceleration.

# APPENDIX C

## Some Computer Programs Useful in the Design
### of Linear Sampled-Data Controllers

In designing linear sampled-data controllers, certain computations are re-quired regardless of the particular application. These computations may be organized into subroutines. Then with a new design problem, one need only code a main program which states the particular details. The subroutines are called to perform the standard computations.

This appendix contains several such subroutines. Program SAMPLSETUP converts a given continuous state space representation of a stochastic process into sampled form. Program SENSLIMDES organizes the explicit design of an op-timal sensor-limited computer control program. It calls subroutine ESTIMATOR to obtain the Kalman state estimator and then subroutine CONTROLLER to ob-tain the Kalman-Koepcke controller. It combines the estimator and controller into an overall state space representation. Finally it can call subroutine STNDRDFORM if one wishes the representation transformed into a minimum arithmetic standard form. Subroutine EVALUATOR computes the mean quad-ratic cost of operating a given control computer program. As an option, this routine will also compute the sequence of the process deviation covariance matrices. This sequence is useful when one wishes to display the time-varia-tion of individual quantities of interest.

Subroutine MINFINDER searches for the minimum of a function of N variables, using the descent method of Davidon. This subroutine is used for finding the best values for the undetermined parameters in a simplified controller design.

The subroutines listed in this appendix are written in a compiler language called MAC. This programming language was developed by the digital com-puter group at the M. I. T. Instrumentation Laboratory. The reader who is familiar with a standard language such as FORTRAN should have no difficulty reading these programs. However, some of the differences between MAC and FORTRAN should be discussed.

159

A statement in MAC may be composed of three lines: an E (exponent) line, a M (main) line, and a S (subscript) line. For example,

```
E           2
M           A
S           I
```

would mean the square of the I-th element in the array A.

Matrix and vector operations can be handled with an explicit notation. For example,

```
E           —
M           A
```

is a vector, and

```
E           *
M           B
```

is a square matrix. The dimension of the vector space is set by a DIMENSION card. A matrix is stored by consecutive rows, so that

```
M           A
S             IN + J
```

refers to the element in the I-th row and J-th column of the N-dimensional matrix A. Indexes in MAC start at zero rather than one.

Differential equations are integrated semi-automatically by MAC using a fourth-order Runge-Kutta numerical method. This facility is used in program SAMPLSETUP. For example, the differential equation relating the state transition matrix A to the fundamental matrix F is written

```
E               *         * *
M             DA/DT = F  A
```

The solutions of the simultaneous differential equations are advanced when the statement

$$M \qquad\qquad DIFEQ \quad T, \quad DT$$

is encountered. One must program a number of passes through a differential equation loop which is an integer multiple of four. According to the Runge-Kutta method, after each group of four passes through the differential equation loop the time T will have been advanced by the increment DT and the dependent variables will have been updated to the new value of T.

Storage or communication between programs of large quantities of data is handled by use of the "datafile." The datafile is kept on the disc storage device and can hold up to 100,000 numbers. The datafile is addressed by the two counters referred to as the file write index and the file read index. One sets the file write index to the location where one wishes to begin writing. A FILE WRITE statement followed by a list of variables causes the numerical values of the variables to be written into consecutive locations in the file. A similar procedure applies for reading numbers from the file.

Certain control statements in MAC have meaning different from FORTRAN. For example DO 9 in MAC means: do statement 9 and then return control to the next statement after the DO statement. This is not like a FORTRAN "do-loop." On the other hand, DO TO 9 FOR I = 1 (1) 10 is similar to a FORTRAN "do-loop."

```
*          JOB 55-238-00 WIDNALL          SAMPLSETUP(D7) PROGRAM BY BILL WIDNALL

*          ESTIMATE 1 MINUTES 500 PRINTLINES

*          USERFILE = DISCFILE

*          MAC* SAMPLSETUP(D7)

M              DIMENSION 7

R              THIS SUBROUTINE CALCULATES THE SAMPLED CHARACTERIZATION OF A CONTINUOUS STOCHASTIC PROCESS.  AS
R              PRESENTLY PROGRAMMED IT IS LIMITED TO A NON-TIME-VARYING PLANT (CONSTANT F AND G MATRICES),
R              A STATIONARY DISTURBANCE (CONSTANT COVN MATRIX), AND A CONSTANT COST WEIGHTING OF THE PROCESS
R              DEVIATION (CONSTANT WX(T), WS(T), WU(T) MATRICES).  FURTHER IT IS LIMITED TO A SINGLE CONTROL VARIABLE.

R              GIVEN THE ABOVE CONSTANT MATRICES FROM THE CALLING PROGRAM TOGETHER WITH THE DESIRED SAMPLE PERIOD,
R              THE ROUTINE COMPUTES THE SAMPLED EQUIVALENT REPRESENTATION BY INTEGRATION OF THE APPROPRIATE
R              DIFFERENTIAL EQUATIONS.  THE INITIAL CONDITION FOR THE STATE TRANSITION MATRIX INTEGRATION IS AN
R              IDENTITY MATRIX.  ALL OTHER ARRAYS HAVE ZERO ARRAYS FOR INITIAL CONDITIONS.

M          RESERVE ZEROS
S              48

M          INDEX J, N

M   ENTER  SUBROUTINE N, DTSAMPLE, NDIFEQ, FILEBASE, SAMPRINT

M          IF N-7 NZ, GO TO ABORTI                           RECOMPILE IF ANOTHER DIMENSION IS WANTED

M          SET FILE READ FILEBASE

E          FILE READ F, G, WX(T), WS(T), WU(T), COVN
M                     * - * -                    *

M          IF SAMPRINT ZERO, GO TO INIT

M          PRINT MSG, SP2

M          DATA INPUT FOR PROGRAM SAMPLSETUP-

M          PRINT HDG

M          N     DTSAMPLE NDIFEQ

M          PRINT N, DTSAMPLE, NDIFEQ, SP2

M          PRINT MSG

M          THE FUNDAMENTAL MATRIX FOR THE PLANT STATE DERIVATIVE IS

M          DO TO PRNTF FOR J=0(1)(N-1)
```

```
E
M      PRNTF     PRINT F
S                        JN
M                PRINT BLANK, SP2

M                PRINT MSG
M                THE CONTROL TO STATE DERIVATIVE ARRAY IS
E
M                PRINT G, SP2

M                PRINT MSG
M                THE CONTINUOUS WEIGHTING MATRIX FOR THE PLANT STATE IS
M                DO TO PRNTWX FOR J=0(1)(N-1)
E
M      PRNTWX    PRINT WX(T)
S                        JN
M                PRINT BLANK, SP2

M                PRINT MSG
M                THE CONTINUOUS WEIGHTING ARRAY FOR STATE AND SIGNAL IS
E
M                PRINT WS(T), SP2

M                PRINT MSG
M                THE CONTINUOUS WEIGHT FOR THE CONTROL SIGNAL IS
M                PRINT WU(T), SP2

M                PRINT MSG
M                THE COVARIANCE MATRIX OF THE PLANT WHITE NOISE DISTURBANCE IS
M                DO TO PRNTCOVN FOR J=0(1)(N-1)
E
M      PRNTCOVN  PRINT COVN
S                        JN
```

```
M            PRINT BLANK, SKIP

M    INIT    DO TO ZEROMAT FOR J=0(1)(NN-1)

M                    ZEROS   = 0
S    ZEROMAT               J

E                *
M            A = ZEROS

M            DO TO INITA FOR J=0(1)(N-1)

M    INITA   A      = 1
S                JN+J

E            -   -
M            B = ZEROS                          STATE TRANSITION MATRIX

E            *   *
M            WX = ZEROS                         CONTROL TO STATE

E            -   -
M            WS = ZEROS                         WEIGHT GIVEN TO STATE

M            WU = C                             CROSS WEIGHT

E            *      *
M            COVZ = ZEROS                       WEIGHT GIVEN TO CONTROL

M            R = 0                              COVARIANCE OF AN INTERVAL DISTURBANCE

M            DT = DTSAMPLE / NDIFEQ             COST DUE TO AN INTERVAL DISTURBANCE

M            T = 0

M            DO TO MDIFEQ FOR M=1(1)(4 NDIFEQ)

E            *       * *
M            DA/DT = F A                        STATE TRANSITION MATRIX

E            -       - -
M            DB/DT = F B + G                    CONTROL TO STATE

E                       *
M            ATRANS = TRANSPOSE(A)

E            *        *     *
M            DWX/DT = ATRANS WX(T) A            WEIGHT GIVEN TO STATE

E            *       -
M            WX(T)B = WX(T) B
```

164

```
E    -           *
M    DWS/DT = ATRANS ( WX(T)B + WS(T) )                              CROSS WEIGHT

E    -          -       *         -         -
M    DWU/DT = B . ( WX(T)B + 2 WS(T) ) + WU(T)                       WEIGHT GIVEN TO CONTROL

E          *  *
M    TEMP = F COVZ

E            *                      *
M    DCOVZ/DT = TEMP + TRANSPOSE(TEMP) + COVN                        COVARIANCE OF AN INTERVAL DISTURBANCE

E          *  *
M    TEMP = WX(T) COVZ

E            N-1
M    DR/DT = SUM ( TEMP     )                                        COST DUE TO AN INTERVAL DISTURBANCE
S            J=0       JN+J

M    MDIFEQ   DIFEQ T, DT

M    IF SAMPRINT ZERO, GO TO FILEND

M    PRINT MSG, SP2

M    INTEGRATION RESULTS FROM PROGRAM SAMPLSETUP-

M    PRINT MSG

M    THE STATE TRANSITION MATRIX FOR THE PLANT IS

M    DO TO PRINTA FOR J=0(1)(N-1)

E             -
M    PRINTA   PRINT A
S                     JN

M    PRINT BLANK, SP2

M    PRINT MSG

M    THE CONTROL TO STATE ARRAY IS

E            -
M    PRINT B, SP2

M    PRINT MSG

M    THE WEIGHTING MATRIX FOR THE SAMPLED PLANT STATE IS
```

```
M        DO TO PRINTWX FOR J=0(1)(N-1)
E
M  PRINTWX  PRINT WX
S                   JN
M        PRINT BLANK, SP2

M        PRINT MSG
M        THE WEIGHTING ARRAY FOR THE CROSSED STATE AND CONTROL IS
E
M        PRINT WS, SP2

M        PRINT MSG
M        THE WEIGHT FOR THE SAMPLED CONTROL IS
M        PRINT WU, SP2

M        PRINT MSG
M        THE COVARIANCE OF AN INTERVAL STATE DISTURBANCE IS
M        DO TO PRINTZ FOR J=0(1)(N-1)
E
M  PRINTZ  PRINT COVZ
S                   JN
M        PRINT BLANK, SP2

M        PRINT MSG
M        THE DIRECT COST IN ONE INTERVAL DUE TO THE PLANT DISTURBANCE IS
M        PRINT R, SP2

M  FILEND  SET FILE WRITE FILEBASE
E
M        FILE WRITE A, B, WX, WS, WU, COVZ, R

M        RETURN
```

166

```
M       ABCRT1   PRINT MSG, SKIP

M       SAMPLSETUP-  THE COMPILED DIMENSION IS NOT COMPATIBLE WITH THE
S                    INPUT DIMENSION.

M       TEMP = SQRT(-1)

M       START AT ENTER

*       ENDJOB
```

167

*     ESTIMATE 1 MINUTES 500 PRINTLINES

*     USERFILE = DISCFILE

*     MAC* SENSLIMDES(D7)

R     THIS SUBROUTINE ORGANIZES THE EXPLICIT DESIGN OF AN OPTIMAL SENSOR LIMITED COMPUTER CONTROL PROGRAM
R     (THAT IS A PROGRAM FOR AN APPLICATION WHERE THE INPUT DATA RATE IS FIXED AND THE CONTROL COMPUTER IS
R     SUFFICIENTLY FAST TO PERFORM THE CONTROL COMPUTATIONS WITHIN ONE SAMPLE PERIOD). THIS EXPLICIT DESIGN
R     IS DUE TO JOSEPH WHO PROVED THAT A KALMAN STATE ESTIMATOR FEEDING A DETERMINISTIC OPTIMAL CONTROLLER
R     IS AN OPTIMAL DESIGN IN AN OVERALL STATISTICAL SENSE.

R     THE ROUTINE USES A SUBROUTINE (ESTIMATOR) TO DESIGN THE REQUIRED KALMAN ESTIMATOR AND ANOTHER
R     SUBROUTINE (CONTROLLER) TO DESIGN THE DETERMINISTIC CONTROLLER. THE ESTIMATOR AND CONTROLLER ARE THEN
R     COMBINED INTO A STATE-SPACE REPRESENTATION CHARACTERIZED BY A SEQUENCE OF STATE TRANSITION MATRICES F,
R     A SEQUENCE OF MEASUREMENT-TO-STATE MATRICES G, A SEQUENCE OF STATE-TO-CONTROL MATRICES H, AND A
R     SEQUENCE OF MEASUREMENT-TO-CONTROL MATRICES D. THESE SEQUENCES ARE PLACED IN THE DATA FILE.

R     IN CERTAIN APPLICATIONS THE USER MAY WISH THE STATE-SPACE REPRESENTATION CONVERTED TO STANDARD FORM.
R     THIS ROUTINE, AS AN OPTION, CAN CALL A SUBROUTINE (STNDRDFORM) TO PERFORM THE DESIRED TRANSFORMATION.

R     AS PRESENTLY PROGRAMMED, THE FORMULAS ARE LIMITED TC PROCESSES HAVING A SINGLE CONTROL ELEMENT AND
R     HAVING EITHER ONE OR TWO ELEMENTS IN THE MEASUREMENT VECTOR.

M     RESERVE IDMAT
S                  48

M     DIMENSION 7

M     INDEX J, K, N

M  ENTER  SUBROUTINE L, N, D, KPBASE,

M              ABASE, BBASE, MBASE, ZBASE, WBASE, XBASE, SBASE,

M              UBASE, MODULO1,     CQBASE,

M              FBASE, GBASE, HBASE, DBASE, MODULO2,

M              ERASEBASE, FORMOPTION, KPRINT, CPRINT, SPRINT, DT

M     IF N-7 NZ, GO TO ABORT1                          RECOMPILE IF ANOTHER DIMENSION IS WANTED

M     KBASE = ERASEBASE,     CBASE = KBASE + N D

M     MODULO3 = N D + N

```
M     CALL ESTIMATOR, L, N, D, KPBASE,
M           ABASE, MBASE, ZBASE, WBASE, MODULO1,
M           KBASE, MODULO3, KPRINT, DT

M     CALL CONTROLLER, L, N, CQBASE,
M           ABASE, BBASE, XBASE, SBASE, UBASE, MODULO1,
M           CBASE, MODULO3, CPRINT, DT

M     DO TO ID FOR J=0(1)(N-1)
M     DO TO ID FOR K=0(1)(N-1)
M     IF J=K, IDMAT    =1, OTHERWISE IDMAT    =0
S                   JN+K                    JN+K
ID

M     DO TO SFILE FOR INTERVAL=0(1)(L-1)
M     SET FILE READ (ABASE + INTERVAL MODULO1)
E
M     FILE READ A*
M     SET FILE READ (BBASE + INTERVAL MODULO1)
E
M     FILE READ B̄
M     SET FILE READ (MBASE + INTERVAL MODULO1)
E
M     IF D=1, FILE READ M̄
E
M     IF D=2, FILE READ M1, M2

M     SET FILE READ (KBASE + INTERVAL MODULO3)
E
M     IF D=1, FILE READ K̄
E
M     IF D=2, FILE READ K1, K2
E
M     FILE READ C̄
```

169

```
E     IF D=1, T* = IDMAT - K̄ M̄
M

E     IF D=2, T* = IDMAT - K1 M1 - K2 M2
M

E     TEMP = Ā - B̄ C
M

E     F = TEMP T̄*
M

E     IF D=1, G = TEMP K̄*
M

E     IF D=2, G1 = TEMP K1, G2 = TEMP K2*
M

E     H = - C̄* T
M

E     IF D=1, D1 = - C̄ · K
M

E     IF D=2, D1 = - C̄ · K1, D2 = - C̄ · K2
M

M     SET FILE WRITE (FBASE + INTERVAL MODULO2)

E     FILE WRITE F*
M

M     SET FILE WRITE (GBASE + INTERVAL MODULO2)

E     IF D=1, FILE WRITE G
M

E     IF D=2, FILE WRITE G1, G2
M

M     SET FILE WRITE (HBASE + INTERVAL MODULO2)

E     FILE WRITE H
M

M     SET FILE WRITE (DBASE + INTERVAL MODULO2)

M     IF D=1, FILE WRITE D1

M  SFILE  IF D=2, FILE WRITE D1, D2

M     IF FORMOPTION ZERO, GO TO SPRINTER
```

M    CALL STNDRDFORM, L, N, D, FBASE, GBASE, HBASE, MODULO2

SPRINTER IF SPRINT ZERO, GO TO SEND

M    PRINT SKIP

M    PRINT MSG, SP4

M    THE STATE SPACE REPRESENTATION OF THE CONTROL PROGRAM-

M    PRINT MSG, SP2

M    THE COMPUTATION TIME

M    PRINT MSG, SP2

M    THE STATE-TO-CONTROL MATRIX H

M    PRINT MSG, SP2

M    THE MEASUREMENT-TO-CONTROL MATRIX D

M    PRINT MSG, SP2

M    THE STATE TRANSITION MATRIX F

M    PRINT MSG, SP2

M    THE MEASUREMENT-TO-STATE MATRIX G (TRANSPOSED)

M    DO TO SPRIN9 FOR INTERVAL=0(1)(L-1)

M    SET FILE READ (FBASE + INTERVAL MODULO2)

E M    FILE READ F *

M    SET FILE READ (GBASE + INTERVAL MODULO2)

E M    IF D=1, FILE READ G

E M    IF D=2, FILE READ G1, G2

M    SET FILE READ (HBASE + INTERVAL MODULO2)

E M    FILE READ H

M    SET FILE READ (DBASE + INTERVAL MODULO2)

```
M           IF D=1, FILE READ D1
M           IF D=2, FILE READ D1, D2
M           PRINT (INTERVAL DT), SP2
E
M           PRINT H, SP2
M           IF D=1, PRINT D1, SP2
M           IF D=2, PRINT D1, D2, SP2
M           DO TO SFPRNT FOR J=0(1)(N-1)
E
M    SFPRNT PRINT F
S               JN
M           PRINT BLANK, SP2
M           IF D=2, GO TO G2PRIN
E
M           PRINT G
M           GO TO SPRIN9
E
M    G2PRIN PRINT G1
E
M           PRINT G2
M    SPRIN9 PRINT BLANK, SP4
M    SEND   RETURN
M    ABORT1 PRINT MSG, SKIP
M    SENSLIMDES-  THE COMPILED DIMENSION IS NOT COMPATIBLE WITH THE
S                 INPUT DIMENSION.
M           TEMP = SQRT(-1)
M           START AT ENTER
*    ENDJOB
```

```
*       JOB 55-238-00 WIDNALL          ESTIMATOR(D7) PROGRAM BY BILL WIDNALL

*       ESTIMATE 1 MINUTES 500 PRINTLINES

*       USERFILE = DISCFILE

*       MAC* ESTIMATOR(D7)

R                INPUTS TO THIS ROUTINE ARE THE INITIAL COVARIANCE MATRIX KP OF THE ESTIMATION ERROR BEFORE THE FIRST
R                MEASUREMENT TOGETHER WITH THE SEQUENCE OF PLANT STATE TRANSITION MATRICES A, THE SEQUENCE OF PLANT
R                STATE-TO-MEASUREMENT MATRICES M, THE SEQUENCE OF COVARIANCE MATRICES Z OF THE PLANT INPUT DISTURBANCE,
R                AND THE SEQUENCE OF COVARIANCE MATRICES W OF THE MEASUREMENT NOISE.

R                GIVEN THESE INPUTS IN THE DATA FILE THIS SUBROUTINE GENERATES THE MINIMUM VARIANCE LINEAR ESTIMATOR FOR
R                THE PLANT STATE (THE KALMAN FILTER) USING THE FORWARD-TIME RECURSION RELATIONS.  THE RESULTING
R                SEQUENCE OF ESTIMATOR GAIN MATRICES K IS PLACED IN THE DATA FILE.

R                AS PRESENTLY PROGRAMMED, THE FORMULAS ARE LIMITED TO PROCESSES HAVING EITHER ONE OR TWO ELEMENTS
R                IN THE MEASUREMENT VECTOR.


M                RESERVE IDMAT
S                        48

M                DIMENSION 7

M                INDEX J, K, N


M       ENTER    SUBROUTINE L, N, D, KPBASE,

M                      ABASE, MBASE, ZBASE, WBASE, MODULO,

M                      KBASE, KMODULO, PRNTCTRL, DT

M                IF N-7 NZ, GO TO ABORT1                             RECOMPILE IF ANOTHER DIMENSION IS WANTED

M                IF PRNTCTRL=0, PBPRNT=0, KPRNT=0, PAPRNT=0

M                IF PRNTCTRL=1, PBPRNT=0, KPRNT=1, PAPRNT=0

M                IF PRNTCTRL=2, PBPRNT=1, KPRNT=1, PAPRNT=0

M                IF PRNTCTRL=3, PBPRNT=1, KPRNT=1, PAPRNT=1


M                IF PRNTCTRL ZERO, GO TO KPINPUT

M                PRINT  SKIP

M                PRINT MSG, SP4

M                FORWARD-TIME RECURSIVE RESULTS FROM PROGRAM ESTIMATOR-
```

```
M          PRINT MSG, SP2
M          THE TIME AT WHICH THE MEASUREMENT IS TAKEN
M          IF PBPRNT ZERO, GO TO KKPRNT1
M          PRINT MSG, SP2
M          THE N BY N ESTIMATION ERROR MATRIX, BEFORE THE MEASUREMENT
M  KKPRNT1  IF KPRNT ZERO, GO TO KPAPRNT1
M          PRINT MSG, SP2
M          THE N BY D OPTIMUM FILTER GAIN MATRIX K  (TRANSPOSED)
M  KPAPRNT1 IF PAPRNT ZERO, GO TO KPINPUT
M          PRINT MSG, SP2
M          THE N BY N ESTIMATION ERROR MATRIX, AFTER THE MEASUREMENT

M  KPINPUT  SET FILE READ KPBASE
E                         *
M          FILE READ KP

M          DO TO ID FOR J=0(1)(N-1)
M          DO TO ID FOR K=0(1)(N-1)
M  ID       IF J=K, IDMAT =1, OTHERWISE IDMAT    =0
S                                          JN+K        JN+K

M          DO TO KEND FOR INTERVAL=0(1)(L-1)
M          SET FILE READ (ABASE + INTERVAL MODULO)
E                       *
M          FILE READ A
M          SET FILE READ (MBASE + INTERVAL MODULO)
E          IF D=1, FILE READ M
M
E          IF D=2, FILE READ M1, M2
M          SET FILE READ (ZBASE + INTERVAL MODULO)
```

```
E     FILE READ *Z
M     SET FILE READ (WBASE + INTERVAL MODULO)

M     IF D=1, FILE READ W

M     IF D=2, FILE READ W11, W12, W21, W22


R     CALCULATE THE OPTIMUM FILTER GAIN MATRIX K, WHICH WILL BE APPLIED TO THE MEASUREMENT DEVIATION FOUND
R     AT THE BEGINNING OF THIS INTERVAL TO DETERMINE THE CORRECTION TO THE ESTIMATE OF THE PLANT STATE.

M     IF D=2, GO TO KD2CALCS

E     KPM = KP M
M

E     TEMP = M . KPM + W
M

E     K = KPM / TEMP
M

E     TEMP = IDMAT - K M
M

E     KWK = K W K
M

M     GO TO KPACALC


E     KD2CALCS KPM1 = KP M1, KPM2 = KP M2
M

E     TEMP11 = M1 . KPM1 + W11, TEMP12 = M1 . KPM2 + W12
M

E     TEMP21 = M2 . KPM1 + W21, TEMP22 = M2 . KPM2 + W22
M

M     DET = TEMP11 TEMP22 - TEMP12 TEMP21

M     INV11 = TEMP22 / DET, INV12 = - TEMP12 / DET

M     INV21 = - TEMP21 / DET, INV22 = TEMP11 / DET

E     K1 = KPM1 INV11 + KPM2 INV21, K2 = KPM1 INV12 + KPM2 INV22
M

E     TEMP = IDMAT - K1 M1 - K2 M2
M
```

175

```
E
M        *    -            -            -            -
       KWK = K1 ( W11 K1 + W12 K2 ) + K2 ( W21 K1 + W22 K2 )

R      CALCULATE THE COVARIANCE OF THE ESTIMATION ERROR AFTER INCORPORATING THE MEASUREMENT.

E
M              *    *      *
KPACALC  KPA = TEMP KP TRANSPOSE(TEMP) + KWK

M        IF PRNTCTRL ZERO, GO TO KCOV1
M        PRINT (INTERVAL DT), SP2
M        IF PBPRNT ZERO, GO TO KKPRNT
M        DO TO PRINTPB FOR J=0(1)(N-1)

E
M                       -
S  PRINTPB  PRINT KP
                      JN
M        PRINT BLANK, SP2

M  KKPRNT  IF KPRNT ZERO, GO TO KPAPRNT
M        IF D=2, GO TO K2PRIN

E
M                 -
M        PRINT K, SP2
M        GO TO KPAPRNT

E
M                 -
M  K2PRIN  PRINT K1
M                 -
M        PRINT K2, SP2

M  KPAPRNT  IF PAPRNT ZERO, GO TO KCOV1
M        DO TO PRINTPA FOR J=0(1)(N-1)

E
M                      -
S  PRINTPA  PRINT KPA
                      JN
M        PRINT BLANK, SP2

R      CALCULATE THE COVARIANCE KP OF THE ERROR IN THE ESTIMATE EXTRAPOLATED TO THE END OF THIS INTERVAL.

E
M            *  *  *
KCOV1  KP = A KPA TRANSPOSE(A) + Z
```

```
M          SET FILE WRITE (KBASE + INTERVAL KMODULO)

E          IF D=1, FILE WRITE K̄
M

E   KEND   IF D=2, FILE WRITE K̄1, K̄2
M

M          IF PBPRNT ZERO, GO TO KRET

M          PRINT (L DT), SP2

M          DO TO PRINTPBT FOR J=0(1)(N-1)

E   PRINTPBT PRINT K̄P
M                   JN
S

M          PRINT BLANK, SP2

M   KRET   RETURN

M   ABORT1 PRINT MSG, SKIP

M   ESTIMATOR-  THE COMPILED DIMENSION IS NOT COMPATIBLE WITH THE
S               INPUT DIMENSION.

M          TEMP = SQRT(-1)

M          START AT ENTER

*   ENDJOB
```

* JOB 55-238-00 WIDNALL          CONTROLLER(D7) PROGRAM BY BILL WIDNALL

* ESTIMATE 1 MINUTES 500 PRINTLINES

* USERFILE = DISCFILE

* MAC* CONTROLLER(D7)

```
R    INPUTS TO THIS ROUTINE ARE THE SEQUENCE OF PLANT STATE TRANSITION MATRICES A, THE SEQUENCE OF CONTROL-
R    TO-PLANT-STATE MATRICES B, THE SEQUENCE OF COST WEIGHTING MATRICES X TO BE APPLIED TO THE PLANT STATE,
R    THE SEQUENCE OF WEIGHTING MATRICES S TO BE APPLIED TO CROSSED STATE AND CONTROL, AND THE SEQUENCE OF
R    WEIGHTING MATRICES U TO BE APPLIED TO THE CONTROL. ALSO SUPPLIED IS THE TERMINAL COST WEIGHTING MATRIX
R    CQ TO BE APPLIED TO THE PLANT STATE AT THE END OF THE FINAL INTERVAL.

R    GIVEN THESE INPUTS IN THE DATA FILE THIS SUBROUTINE GENERATES THE MINIMUM QUADRATIC COST COMPUTER
R    CONTROL PROGRAM USING THE BACKWARD-TIME RECURSION RELATIONS.  THE RESULTING SEQUENCE OF CONTROL PROGRAM
R    GAIN MATRICES C IS PLACED IN THE DATA FILE.

R    AS PRESENTLY PROGRAMMED, THE FORMULAS ARE LIMITED TO PROBLEMS HAVING A SINGLE CONTROL VARIABLE.


M    DIMENSION 7

M    INDEX J, N


M ENTER    SUBROUTINE L, N, CQBASE,

M                       ABASE, BBASE, XBASE, SBASE, UBASE, MODULO,

M                       CBASE, CMODULO, PRNTCTRL, DT          RECOMPILE IF ANOTHER DIMENSION IS WANTED

M    IF N-7 NZ, GO TO ABORT0

M    IF PRNTCTRL=0, CQPRNT=0, CPRNT=0

M    IF PRNTCTRL=1, CQPRNT=0, CPRNT=1

M    IF PRNTCTRL=2, CQPRNT=1, CPRNT=1


M    IF PRNTCTRL ZERO, GO TO CQINPUT

M    PRINT SKIP

M    PRINT MSG, SP4

M    BACKWARD-TIME RECURSIVE RESULTS FROM PROGRAM CONTROLLER-

M    PRINT MSG, SP2

M    THE TIME OF THE BEGINNING OF THE CONTROL INTERVAL
```

```
M        IF CQPRNT ZERO, GO TO CCPRNT1

M        PRINT MSG, SP2

M        THE N BY N COST MATRIX AT THE END OF THE CONTROL INTERVAL

M   CCPRNT1   IF CPRNT ZERO, GO TO CQINPUT

M        PRINT MSG, SP2

M        THE N OPTIMUM CONTROL GAINS C FOR THE PLANT STATE AT THE
S        BEGINNING OF THE CONTROL INTERVAL

M   CQINPUT   SET FILE READ CQBASE

E                       *
M        FILE READ CQ

M        DO TO CEND FOR INTERVAL=(L-1)(-1)0

M        SET FILE READ (ABASE + INTERVAL MODULO )

E                  *
M        FILE READ A

M        SET FILE READ (BBASE + INTERVAL MODULO)

E                  ‾
M        FILE READ B

M        SET FILE READ (XBASE + INTERVAL MODULO)

E                  *
M        FILE READ X

M        SET FILE READ (SBASE + INTERVAL MODULO)

E                  ‾
M        FILE READ S

M        SET FILE READ (UBASE + INTERVAL MODULO)

M        FILE READ U

R        CALCULATE THE OPTIMUM CONTROL GAIN MATRIX C, WHICH WILL BE APPLIED TO THE PLANT STATE AT THE BEGINNING
R        OF THIS INTERVAL TO DETERMINE THE CONSTANT CONTROL TO BE HELD DURING THIS INTERVAL.

E          ‾   *
M        BCQ = B CQ
```

```
E          TEMP = BCQ . B
M          IF TEMP NEG, GO TO ABORT1
M          TEMP = TEMP + U
M          IF TEMP ZERO, GO TO ABORT2
E
M          C = (1/TEMP)( BCQ A + S )
M          IF PRNTCTRL ZERO, GO TO CQUAD1
M          PRINT (INTERVAL DT), SP2
M          IF CQPRNT ZERO, GO TO CCPRNT
M          DO TO PRINTCQ FOR J=0(1)(N-1)
E
M  PRINTCQ PRINT CQ
S                  JN
M          PRINT BLANK, SP2
M  CCPRNT  IF CPRNT ZERO, GO TO CQUAD1
E
M          PRINT C, SP2
R          CALCULATE THE QUADRATIC FORM OPTIMUM COST MATRIX FROM THE BACKWARD RECURSION RELATION.
E                      *   -   -
M  CQUAD1  TEMP = A - B C
E                  *   -
M          TEM = C S
E              *  -   -      *                      *
M          TEM = C U C - TEM - TRANSPOSE(TEM) + X
E                 *              *     *
M          CQ = TRANSPOSE(TEMP) CQ TEMP + TEM
M          SET FILE WRITE (CBASE + INTERVAL CMODULO)
E                         -
M  CEND    FILE WRITE C
```

180

```
M          IF CQPRNT ZERO, GO TO CRET

M          PRINT (- DT), SP2

M          DO TO PRINTCQT FOR J=0(1)(N-1)

E
M   PRINTCQT PRINT CQ
S                   NJ

M          PRINT BLANK, SP2

    CRET   RETURN

M   ABORT0  PRINT MSG, SKIP

M   CONTROLLER-  THE COMPILED DIMENSION IS NOT COMPATIBLE WITH THE
S                INPUT DIMENSION.

M          TEMP = SQRT(-1)

M   ABORT1  PRINT MSG, SKIP

M          THE QUADRATIC FORM CCST MATRIX IS NEGATIVE.

M          TEMP = SQRT(-1)

M   ABORT2  PRINT MSG, SKIP

E          THE FEEDBACK CALCULATIONS HAVE LEAD TO A DIVIDE-BY-ZERO.
M          THE FEEDBACK GAINS ARE INDETERMINATE.  TRY ADDING A CONTROL
S          PENALTY.

M          TEMP = SQRT(-1)

M          START AT ENTER

*   ENDJOB
```

JOB 55-238-00 WIDNALL          STNDRDFORM(D7) PROGRAM BY BILL WIDNALL

```
*     JOB 55-238-00 WIDNALL          STNDRDFORM(D7) PROGRAM BY BILL WIDNALL

*     ESTIMATE 1 MINUTES 500 PRINTLINES

*     USERFILE = DISCFILE

*     MAC* STNDRDFORM(D7)

R       THIS SUBROUTINE COMPUTES A STANDARD FORM TIME-VARYING STATE-SPACE REPRESENTATION, WHICH IS EQUIVALENT
R     WITH RESPECT TO INPUT-OUTPUT BEHAVIOR TO THE GIVEN ARBITRARY STATE-SPACE REPRESENTATION.
R     THE USEFULNESS OF THIS STANDARD FORM IS THAT THE NUMBER OF NON-ZERO COEFFICIENTS GROWS ONLY LINEARLY
R     WITH THE DIMENSION OF THE STATE SPACE, WHILE FOR THE ARBITRARY REPRESENTATION THE NUMBER OF
R     COEFFICIENTS GROWS AS THE SQUARE OF THE DIMENSION OF THE STATE SPACE.

R       THE INPUT TO THIS ROUTINE IS THE GIVEN STATE-SPACE REPRESENTATION- THE SEQUENCE OF STATE TRANSITION
R     MATRICES F, THE SEQUENCE OF INPUT-TO-STATE MATRICES G, AND THE SEQUENCE OF STATE-TO-OUTPUT MATRICES H.

R       GIVEN THESE INPUTS IN THE DATA FILE THIS ROUTINE GENERATES THE REQUIRED TIME-VARYING STATE-SPACE
R     TRANSFORMATION T USING A BACKWARD-TIME RECURSION RELATION. THE DESIRED SEQUENCE OF STANDARD FORM
R     INPUT-TO-STATE MATRICES P AND SEQUENCE OF STANDARD FORM BOTTOM-ROWS Q FOR THE STATE TRANSITION
R     MATRICES ARE THEN COMPUTED. THE STANDARD FORM STATE SPACE REPRESENTATION IS THEN WRITTEN IN THE
R     DATA FILE.

R       AS PRESENTLY PROGRAMMED, THE STANDARD FORM CAN BE COMPUTED ONLY FOR PROBLEMS HAVING A SINGLE
R     OUTPUT ELEMENT AND HAVING EITHER ONE OR TWO ELEMENTS IN THE MEASUREMENT VECTOR.

M         RESERVE ZEROS , T
S                        6    48

M         DIMENSION 7

M         INDEX J, K, N

M ENTER   SUBROUTINE L, N, D, FBASE, GBASE, HBASE, MODULO

M         IF N-7 NZ, GO TO ABORT1

M         DO TO SINIT FOR J=0(1)(NN-1)

M SINIT   T = 0
S              J

M         DO TO ZEROVEC FOR J=0(1)(N-1)

M ZEROVEC ZEROS = 0
S              J

M         DO TO SEND FOR INTERVAL = (L-1)(-1)0           RECOMPILE IF ANOTHER DIMENSION IS WANTED

M         SET FILE READ (FBASE + INTERVAL MODULO)
```

182

```
E  M   FILE READ  F*

   M   SET FILE READ (GBASE + INTERVAL MODULO)

E  M   IF D=1, FILE READ  G̅

E  M   IF D=2, FILE READ  G̅1,  G2

   M   SET FILE READ (HBASE + INTERVAL MODULO)

E  M   FILE READ  H̅

E  M   IF D=1,  P̅ = *T̅  G̅

E  M   IF D=2,  P1 = T̅  G̅1,  P2 = *T̅  G̅2

E  M   T̅NTH = T̅
   S              (N-1)N

   M   DO TO TRECURS FOR  J=(N-2)(-1)0

E  M   TRECURS   T̅      = T̅    *F̅
   S             (J+1)N    JN

E  M   T̅ = H̅

E  M   IF INTERVAL+1+N-L PNZ, Q=ZEROS, GO TO SFILE

E  M   CALL DPMATINV, N, T*

E  M   RESUME BADBIT, TINV

   M   IF BADBIT=1, GO TO ABORT

E  M   Q̅ = T̅NTH  F̅  **TINV

R      IN THE STANDARD FORM STATE TRANSITION MATRIX F THE UPPER LEFT (N-1) BY 1 PARTITION IS ALL ZEROS, THE
R      UPPER RIGHT (N-1) BY (N-1) PARTITION IS AN IDENTITY MATRIX, AND THE BOTTOM ROW IS THE ARRAY Q.
R      THE STANDARD FORM INPUT-TO-STATE MATRIX G IS GIVEN BY P.  IN THE STANDARD FORM STATE-TO-OUTPUT ARRAY H,
R      THE FIRST ELEMENT IS UNITY AND ALL THE OTHERS ARE ZERO.
```

183

```
M    SFILE        DO TO F1 FOR J=0(1)(N-2)

M                 F   = 0
S                  JN

M                 DO TO F2 FOR J=0(1)(N-2)

M                 DO TO F2 FOR K=1(1)(N-1)

M    F2           IF K=J+1, F      = 1 , OTHERWISE F      = 0
S                           NJ+K                    NJ+K

E                 _      _
M                 F     = Q
S                  (N-1)N

E                 _
M                 H = ZEROS

M                 H  = 1
S                  0

M                 SET FILE WRITE (FBASE + INTERVAL MODULO)

E                              *
M                 FILE WRITE F

M                 SET FILE WRITE (GBASE + INTERVAL MODULO)

E                              _
M                 IF D=1, FILE WRITE P

E                              _       _
M                 IF D=2, FILE WRITE P1, P2

M                 SET FILE WRITE (HBASE + INTERVAL MODULO)

E                            _
M    SEND         FILE WRITE H

M                 RETURN

M    ABORT1       PRINT MSG, SKIP

M    STNDRDFORM-  THE COMPILED DIMENSION IS NOT COMPATIBLE WITH THE
S                 INPUT DIMENSION.

M                 TEMP = SQRT(-1)
```

184

```
M     ABORT     PRINT MSG, SKIP
M     STNDRDFORM- DPMATINV REPORTS A BAD INVERSE.
M     TEMP = SQRT(-1)

M     START AT ENTER
*     ENDJOB
```

```
*        JOB 55-238-00 WIDNALL        EVALUATOR(D7) PROGRAM BY BILL WIDNALL

*        ESTIMATE 1 MINUTES 500 PRINTLINES

*        USERFILE = DISCFILE

*        MAC* EVALUATOR(D7)

R        THIS SUBROUTINE HELPS EVALUATE A GIVEN LINEAR COMPUTER CONTROL PROGRAM.  IT COMPUTES THE MEAN QUADRATIC
R        COST OF OPERATING THE GIVEN PROGRAM OVER THE CONTROL PROCESS PERIOD.  AS AN OPTION, THIS ROUTINE WILL
R        FILE THE SEQUENCE OF THE PROCESS DEVIATION COVARIANCE MATRICES.  THIS SEQUENCE IS USEFUL WHEN ONE
R        WISHES TO DISPLAY THE TIME-VARIATION OF INDIVIDUAL QUANTITIES OF INTEREST.

R        THE ROUTINE IS COMPILED TO HANDLE A PLANT STATE SPACE OF DIMENSION N AS GIVEN IN THE DIMENSION
R        STATEMENT.  THE COMPUTER CONTROL PROGRAM STATE SPACE CAN BE OF ANY DIMENSION M FROM 1 TO N.
R        FOR PROGRAMMING CONVENIENCE, IF M IS LESS THAN N THE ROUTINE AUGMENTS THE CONTROL PROGRAM STATE
R        SPACE REPRESENTATION IN SUCH A WAY THAT THE CONTROL PROGRAM DIMENSION EQUALS THE PLANT DIMENSION.

R        AS PRESENTLY WRITTEN, THIS ROUTINE IS LIMITED TO PROCESSES HAVING A SINGLE CONTROL ELEMENT AND HAVING
R        EITHER ONE OR TWO ELEMENTS IN THE MEASUREMENT VECTOR.

M        RESERVE ZEROS
S            48

M        DIMENSION 7

M        INDEX I, M, N

M  ENTER  SUBROUTINE L, N, M, D,  KPBASE,  ABASE,  BBASE, MBASE,

M                    ZBASE, WBASE, XBASE, SBASE, UBASE, RBASE, MODULO1,

M                    CQBASE,  FBASE, GBASE, HBASE, CBASE, MODULO2,

M                    EBASE, MODULO3,  EMODE

M         IF N-7 NZ, GO TO ABORT1                        RECOMPILE IF ANOTHER DIMENSION IS WANTED

M         DO TO ZEROMAT FOR I=0(1)(NN-1)

M  ZEROMAT ZEROS  = 0
S            I

R         AUGMENT THE COMPUTER STATE SPACE ARRAYS WITH ZEROS-

E         * - *
M         F = ZEROS
```

```
E   IF D=1, G̅ = ZEROS
M

E   IF D=2, G̅1 = ZEROS, G̅2 = ZEROS
M

E   H̅ = ZEROS
M

R   IN THE INITIAL COVARIANCE MATRIX OF THE COMBINED PLANT-COMPUTER STATE SPACE, THE UPPER LEFT PARTITION
R   IS THE INITIAL COVARIANCE OF THE PLANT STATE.  THE OTHER PARTITIONS ARE ZERO.

M   SET FILE READ KPBASE

E                *
M   FILE READ COVS11

E        *                *                *
M   COVS12=ZEROS, COVS21=ZEROS, COVS22=ZEROS

R   THE MEAN VALUE OF THE COST FOR ZERO INTERVAL CONTROL PROCESSES IS-

M   EC = 0

M   DO TO ENDPROG FOR INTERVAL = 0(1)(L-1)

R   FROM THE DATA FILE READ THE SET OF ARRAYS DESCRIBING THE PLANT DYNAMICS, THE RANDOM DISTURBANCES, AND
R   THE COST WEIGHTS OVER THE PRESENT INTERVAL.  ALSO READ THE SET OF ARRAYS DESCRIBING THE CONTROL PROGRAM
R   COMPUTATIONS FOR THE BEGINNING OF THE PRESENT INTERVAL.

M   SET FILE READ (ABASE + INTERVAL MODULO1)

E            *
M   FILE READ A                                PLANT STATE TRANSITION MATRIX

E   SET FILE READ (BBASE + INTERVAL MODULO1)
M

E            _
M   FILE READ B                                CONTROL-TO-PLANT-STATE MATRIX

M   SET FILE READ (MBASE + INTERVAL MODULO1)

E                    _
M   IF D=1, FILE READ M

E
M   IF D=2, FILE READ M1, M2

M   SET FILE READ (ZBASE + INTERVAL MODULO1)   PLANT-STATE-TO-MEASUREMENT MATRIX
```

187

```
E
M     FILE READ Z*                                    PLANT-DISTURBANCE COVARIANCE MATRIX
M     SET FILE READ (WBASE + INTERVAL MODULO1)
M     IF D=1, FILE READ W                             MEASUREMENT NOISE COVARIANCE MATRIX
M     IF D=2, FILE READ W11, W12, W21, W22
M     SET FILE READ (XBASE + INTERVAL MODULO1)
E
M     FILE READ X*                                    PLANT-STATE COST WEIGHT MATRIX
M     SET FILE READ (SBASE + INTERVAL MODULO1)
E
M     FILE READ S̄                                     PLANT-STATE AND CONTROL WEIGHT MATRIX
M     SET FILE READ (UBASE + INTERVAL MODULO1)
M     FILE READ U                                     CONTROL WEIGHT
M     SET FILE READ (RBASE + INTERVAL MODULO1)
M     FILE READ R                                     COST OF THE INTERVAL DISTURBANCE

M     SET FILE READ (FBASE + INTERVAL MODULO2)
M     I = 0
M
S     FIN   FILE READ $F_{IN}$ TO $F_{IN+M-1}$        COMPUTER STATE TRANSITION MATRIX
M     I=I+1, IF I-M NEG, GO TO FIN
M     SET FILE READ (GBASE + INTERVAL MODULO2)
M
S     IF D=1, FILE READ $G_0$ TO $G_{M-1}$
M
S     IF D=2, FILE READ $G1_0$ TO $G1_{M-1}$, $G2_0$ TO $G2_{M-1}$   MEASUREMENT-TO-COMPUTOR-STATE MATRIX
M     SET FILE READ (HBASE + INTERVAL MODULO2)
M
S     FILE READ $H_0$ TO $H_{M-1}$
M     SET FILE READ (CBASE + INTERVAL MODULO2)        COMPUTER-STATE-TO-CONTROL MATRIX
M     IF D=1, FILE READ C
M     IF D=2, FILE READ C1, C2                        MEASUREMENT-TO-CONTROL MATRIX
```

188

```
E M    IF D=1, C̄M̄ = C̄ M̄

E M    IF D=2, C̄M̄ = C̄1 M̄1 + C̄2 M̄2

  M    IF EMODE ZERO, GO TO ECCALC

R R    WHEN EMODE IS NON-ZERO, COMPUTE AND FILE THE PROCESS DEVIATION (PLANT-STATE AND CONTROL) COVARIANCE
       MATRIX.

E M    COVE12 = COVS11 C̄M̄* + COVS12 H̄

E M    COVE21 = C̄M̄ COVS11 + H̄ COVS21*

E M    TEMP22 = C̄M̄ COVS12 + H̄ COVS22*

E M    TEM22 = COVE21 . C̄M̄ + TEMP22 . H̄

  M    IF D=1, COVE22 = TEM22 + C̄ W C̄

  M    IF D=2, COVE22 = TEM22 + C̄1 W11 C̄1 + C̄1 C̄2 (W12+W21) +C̄2 W22 C̄2

  M    SET FILE WRITE (EBASE + INTERVAL MODULO3)

  M    I = 0

M S    EFILE   FILE WRITE COVS11     TO COVS11      , COVE12
                          IN           IN+N-1              I

  M    I=I+1, IF I-N NEG, GO TO EFILE

E M    FILE WRITE COVE21, COVE22


R R    ADD THE MEAN COST OF THE PRESENT CONTROL INTERVAL TO THE RUNNING TOTAL MEAN COST OF THE
       CONTROL PROCESS-

E M    ECCALC   TEMP = S̄ C̄M̄ ,   CMU = C̄M̄* Ū

E M    R11 = X̄ + TEMP + TRANSPOSE(TEMP) + CMU C̄M̄

E M    R12 = S̄ H̄ + CMU H̄

E M    R21 = TRANSPOSE(R12)
```

189

E M
S
M
M
M

R R

E M
E M
E M
E M
E M
E M
E M
E M
E M
E M

$$R22 = \overline{H} \, U \, \overline{H}$$

$$TEMP = R11 \; \overline{COVS11} + R12 \; \overline{COVS21}$$

$$TEMP = TEMP + R21 \; \overline{COVS12} + R22 \; \overline{COVS22}$$

$$TR(RS) = \sum_{I=0}^{N-1} ( \; TEMP_{IN+I} \; )$$

IF D=1, $TR(YD) = \overline{C} \, U \, C \, \overline{W}$

IF D=2, $TR(YD) = C1 \, U \, \overline{C1} \; W11 + C1 \, U \, C2 \; (W21+W12) + C2 \, U \, \overline{C2} \; W22$

$$EC = EC + TR(RS) + TR(YD) + R$$

THE COVARIANCE MATRIX OF THE COMBINED STATE AT THE NEXT CONTROL INTERVAL IS CALCULATED BY THE RECURSION RELATION—

$$T11 = \overline{A} + \overline{B} \; CM$$

$$T12 = \overline{B} \; \overline{H}$$

IF D=1, $T21 = \overline{G} \; \overline{M}$

IF D=2, $T21 = G1 \; \overline{M1} + G2 \; \overline{M2}$

$$TEMP11 = TRANSPOSE(\overline{T11})$$

$$TEMP12 = TRANSPOSE(\overline{T21})$$

$$TEMP21 = TRANSPOSE(\overline{T12})$$

$$TEMP22 = TRANSPOSE(\overline{F})$$

$$TEM11 = COVS11 \; \overline{TEMP11} + COVS12 \; \overline{TEMP21}$$

$$TEM12 = COVS11 \; \overline{TEMP12} + COVS12 \; \overline{TEMP22}$$

$$TEM21 = COVS21 \; \overline{TEMP11} + COVS22 \; \overline{TEMP21}$$

```
        *        *                   *
TEM22 = COVS21 TEMP12 + COVS22 TEMP22

        *                *
COVS11 = T11 TEM11 + T12 TEM21

        *                *
COVS12 = T11 TEM12 + T12 TEM22

        *             *
COVS21 = T21 TEM11 + F TEM21

        *             *
COVS22 = T21 TEM12 + F TEM22

IF D=2, GO TO LDL2

_    _ _
BC = B C

        *    _    *
TEM11 = BC W BC + Z

        *    _
TEM12 = BC W G

                 *
TEM21 = TRANSPOSE(TEM12)

        _   _
TEM22 = G W G

GO TO SNEXT

LDL2    _   _ _       _   _ _
        BC1 = B C1,  BC2 = B C2

        _             _
TEMP11 = BC1 W11 + BC2 W21

        _             _
TEMP12 = BC1 W12 + BC2 W22

        _           _
TEMP21 = G1 W11 + G2 W21

        _           _
TEMP22 = G1 W12 + G2 W22

        *                 _                *
TEM11 = TEMP11 BC1 + TEMP12 BC2 + Z

        _              _
TEM12 = TEMP11 G1 + TEMP12 G2
```

```
E          *
M   TEM21 = TRANSPOSE(TEM12)

E          -        -        -
M   TEM22 = TEMP21 G1 + TEMP22 G2

E                  *        *
M   SNEXT   COVS11 = COVS11 + TEM11

E                  *        *
M           COVS12 = COVS12 + TEM12

E                  *        *
M           COVS21 = COVS21 + TEM21

E                  *        *
M   ENDPROG  COVS22 = COVS22 + TEM22


M   IF EMODE ZERO, GO TO ECTCALC

R   WHEN EMODE IS NON-ZERO, FILE THE TERMINAL PLANT-STATE COVARIANCE MATRIX-

M   SET FILE WRITE (EBASE + L MODULO3)

E          *
M   FILE WRITE COVS11


R   THE MEAN VALUE OF THE COST FOR THE ENTIRE CONTROL PROCESS IS-

M   ECTCALC SET FILE READ CQBASE

E          *
M   FILE READ R11

E          *    *
V   TEMP = R11 COVS11

E                  N-1
M   TR(RS) = SUM ( TEMP   )
S               I=0      IN+I

M   EC = EC + TR(RS)


M   RETURN EC


M   ABORT1  PRINT MSG, SKIP
```

```
M   EVALUATOR-  THE COMPILED DIMENSION IS NOT COMPATIBLE WITH THE
S               INPUT DIMENSION.

M   TEMP = SQRT(-1)

M   START AT ENTER

*   ENDJOB
```

```
*        JOB 55-238-00 WIDNALL        MINFINDER SUBROUTINE BY BILL WIDNALL

*        ESTIMATE 1 MINUTES 500 PRINTLINES

*        USERFILE = DISCFILE

*        MAC* MINFINDER

R        THIS SUBROUTINE USES THE METHOD OF DAVIDON TO FIND THE MINIMUM OF A FUNCTION OF N VARIABLES.  ONE
R        MUST PROVIDE AS A SEPARATE SUBROUTINE THE COMPUTATIONS WHICH EVALUATE THE FUNCTION FOR A GIVEN CHOICE
R        OF THE VARIABLES.  INPUTS TO THIS SUBROUTINE ARE-   (N) THE NUMBER OF VARIABLES OF THE FUNCTION,
R        (DL) THE NUMERICAL DIFFERENCING INTERVAL USED TO ESTIMATE THE GRADIENT, (CRITERION) THE SMALL STEP
R        SIZE WHICH WILL BE ACCEPTED AS INDICATION OF CONVERGENCE, (LOWBOUND) A LOWER BOUND ESTIMATE OF THE
R        MINIMUM VALUE OF THE FUNCTION, (MAXCALLS) AND (MAXITER) THE MAXIMUM NUMBER OF CALLS TO THE FUNCTION
R        SUBROUTINE AND THE MAXIMUM NUMBER OF ITERATIONS OF THE DAVIDON METHOD WHICH CAN BE ALLOWED WITH THE
R        AVAILABLE COMPUTER TIME, AND FINALLY THE VALUES OF THE N VARIABLES AT WHICH THE SEARCH FOR THE MINIMUM
R        IS TO BEGIN.

M        RESERVE H , X , G(X) , S , U , TEMP , SIG , G(X-SIG) , Y , HY
S                 99   9   9     9   9   9      9     9          9   9

M        INDEX N, I, J, K


M  ENTER SUBROUTINE

M        READ N, DL, CRITERION, LOWBOUND, MAXCALLS, MAXITER

M        PRINT HDG

M        N      DL     CRITERION LOWBOUND  MAXCALLS  MAXITER

M        PRINT N, DL, CRITERION, LOWBOUND, MAXCALLS, MAXITER, SP2

M        READ X TO X
S              0  N-1

M        PRINT MSG

M        THE INITIAL N ELEMENTS OF X

M        PRINT X TO X , SP4
S              0   N-1

M        IF N-10 PNZ, GO TO ABORT2

R        THE FIRST CALL TO THE FUNCTION IS FOR INITIALIZATION PURPOSES.
```

```
M      CALL FUNCTION

R      THE INITIAL VALUE ASSUMED FOR THE H MATRIX IS THE IDENTITY MATRIX.

M      DO TO HINIT FOR I=0(1)(N-1)

M      DO TO HINIT FOR K=0(1)(N-1)

M      HINIT  IF K=I, H    =1, OTHERWISE H    =0
S                     NI+K                NI+K

R      COMPUTE THE FUNCTION AND ITS GRADIENT AT X.

M      NCALL = C

M      CALL FUNCTION, X   TO X
S                      0      N-1

M      RESUME F(X)

M      NCALL = NCALL + 1

M      PRINT MSG

M      THE INITIAL VALUE OF THE FUNCTION IS COMPUTED TO BE

M      PRINT F(X), SP2

M      DO GRADIENT

M      ITERATION = 0
```

```
M    HEADING   ITERATION = ITERATION + 1 ,  NSTEP = 0

M              PRINT MSG, SP2

M              BEGIN A NEW ITERATION.

M              PRINT MSG

M              THE GRADIENT OF THE FUNCTION AT X IS-

M              PRINT G(X)   TO G(X)    , SP2
S                       0        N-1

M              PRINT MSG

M              THE ESTIMATE OF THE INVERSE OF THE MATRIX OF SECOND PARTIALS IS-

M              DO TO HPRINT FOR I=0(1)(N-1)

M    HPRINT    PRINT H     TO H
S                     NI      NI+N-1

M              PRINT SP2

M              PRINT MSG

M              THE ESTIMATE OF THE STEP REQUIRED TO REACH THE MINIMUM IS-

M              DO TO ESTSTEP FOR I=0(1)(N-1)

E                         N-1
M    ESTSTEP   S   = - SUM( H      G(X) )
S               I      K=0   NI+K     K

M              PRINT S    TO S    , SP2
S                     0       N-1

M              PRINT MSG

M              RETAIN THE DIRECTION OF THE ESTIMATED STEP AS A UNIT VECTOR-

E                          N-1    2
M    SMAG = SQRT( SUM( S   ) )
S                          I=0    I

M              DO TO SUNIT FOR I=0(1)(N-1)

M    SUNIT     U   = S   / SMAG
S               I     I

M              PRINT U    TO U    , SP2
S                     0       N-1
```

M     PRINT MSG, SP2

M
S     WE NOW PROCEED TO FIND THE MINIMUM VALUE OF THE FUNCTION ALONG
    THE LINE FROM X IN THE DIRECTION GIVEN BY THE UNIT VECTOR.

M     PRINT HDG

M     ITERATION NSTEP    TRIAL    L     STEP    F(L+STEP)

R     FOR THE PROCEDURE TO BE STABLE, THE UNIT VECTOR MUST NOT BE DIRECTED UPHILL.

E
M
S     $DF/DL = \sum_{I=0}^{N-1}( G(X)_I U_I )$

M     IF DF/DL POS, GO TO ABORT1

M     L=0, F(L)=F(X)

R
R
R     AFTER N OR MORE ITERATIONS THE VECTOR S CONVERGES TO THE ACTUAL STEP REQUIRED TO REACH THE MINIMUM.
    MEANWHILE IT IS REASONABLE TO LIMIT THE STEP TO ONE EQUAL TO THAT REQUIRED FOR A PARABOLA HAVING
    A VALUE F(L) AND A SLOPE DF/DL AT THE POINT L AND HAVING A MINIMUM VALUE OF LOWBOUND.

M     STEPMAX = - 2 ( F(L) - LOWBOUND ) / DF/DL

M     STEP = MINIMUM( SMAG, STEPMAX )

R
R     THE FUNCTION IS THEN EVALUATED BY THE STEP. IF THE TRIAL FAILS (THAT IS INCREASES
    ORDER OF MAGNITUDE AND TRY AGAIN. REPEAT UNTIL A TRIAL SUCCEEDS.

M     NSTEP=NSTEP+1, TRIAL=0

M     STEP1    IF-NCALL-MAXCALLS POS, GO TO ENDITER

M     TRIAL = TRIAL + 1

M     DO TO CALL1 FOR I=C(1)(N-1)

M
S     CALL1    $TEMP_I = X_I + (L+STEP)U_I$ , I=0 to N-1

M
S     CALL FUNCTION, TEMP TO TEMP

M     RESUME F(L+STEP)

M     NCALL = NCALL + 1

M     PRINT ITERATION, NSTEP, TRIAL, L, STEP, F(L+STEP)

```
M       IF F(L+STEP)-F(L) PNZ, STEP=.1STEP, GO TO STEP1

M       L1=L,    F(L1)=F(L)

M       L=L+STEP, F(L)=F(L+STEP)

M       OLDSTEP=STEP

R       LOOK FOR A THIRD POINT IN THE VICINITY OF L.   ACCORDING TO ROSENBROCK,  A  GOOD  STEP  TO  TRY  IS
R       TRIPLE THE PREVIOUS SUCCESSFUL STEP.

M  ROSEN   STEP = 3 OLDSTEP

R       DO NOT ALLOW STEPS TO NEGATIVE L.

M       IF L+STEP NEG, STEP = -.5 L

R       TRY THE INDICATED STEP.  IF THE TRIAL FAILS, CUT THE STEP SIZE IN HALF AND REVERSE THE DIRECTION.
R       REPEAT UNTIL A TRIAL SUCCEEDS OR UNTIL CONVERGENCE HAS BEEN PROVED.

M  NEXTSTEP NSTEP=NSTEP+1,     TRIAL=0

M  STEPR   IF NCALL-MAXCALLS POS, GO TO ENDITER

M       TRIAL = TRIAL + 1

M       DO TO CALLR FOR I=C(1)(N-1)

M  CALLR   TEMP  = X  + (L+STEP)U
S              I    I             I

M       CALL FUNCTION, TEMP  TO TEMP
S                          O        N-1

M       RESUME F(L+STEP)

M       NCALL = NCALL + 1

M       PRINT ITERATION, NSTEP, TRIAL, L, STEP, F(L+STEP)

R       A SUCCESS IS WHEN A TRIAL RESULT IS LESS THAN OR EQUAL TO THE PREVIOUSLY KNOWN LOWEST POINT.

M       IF F(L+STEP) - F(L) NOPZ, GO TO NEWPOINT

R       DO NOT CONTINUE TO SEARCH FOR A NEW SUCCESS IF IT HAS BEEN ESTABLISHED THAT THE MINIMUM LIES WITHIN
R       THE CRITERION DISTANCE OF THE LAST SUCCESS.
```

198

```
M    IF ABS(STEP)-.5 CRITERION NEG, IF TRIAL-3 POS, GO TO ENDITER

R    OTHERWISE CONTINUE THE SEARCH BY ALTERNATELY LOOKING ON EACH SIDE OF THE LAST SUCCESS WHILE CUTTING
R    THE TRIAL STEP SIZE BY HALF.

M    STEP = -.5 STEP
M    IF ABS(STEP) - ABS(.5 OLDSTEP) POS, STEP = -.5 OLDSTEP
M    GO TO STEPR

M    NEWPOINT L2=L1,    F(L2)=F(L1)
M             L1=L,     F(L1)=F(L)
M    L=L+STEP, F(L)=F(L+STEP)
M    OLDSTEP=STEP

R    TERMINATE THE MINIMIZATION ALONG THIS DIRECTION IF THE LAST SUCCESSFUL STEP IS LESS THAN THE CRITERION.
M    IF ABS(STEP)-CRITERION NEG, GO TO ENDITER

R    THE SECOND DIFFERENCE ITERATION FORMULA CONVERGES TO THE MINIMUM BY TAKING EACH STEP TO THE EXACT
R    LOCATION OF THE MINIMUM OF A PARABOLA PASSING THROUGH THE LAST THREE POINTS.
M    DIFF1 = F(L)/(L-L1) + F(L1)/(L1-L)
M    DIFF2 = F(L)/(L-L1)(L-L2) + F(L1)/(L1-L)(L1-L2)
M          + F(L2)/(L2-L)(L2-L1)

R    FOR THE METHOD TO WORK, THE CURVE MUST BE CONCAVE UPWARD.  THEREFORE IF THE SECOND DIFFERENCE IS
R    NEGATIVE OR ZERO, GO BACK TO THE ROSENBROCK DESCENT METHOD (AND IGNORE BOTH DIVIDED DIFFERENCES).
M    IF DIFF2 NORZ, GO TO ROSEN

R    BY THE PARABOLIC METHOD, THE REQUIRED STEP IS
M    STEP = ( L1 - L ) / 2 - DIFF1 / 2 DIFF2

R    HOWEVER FOR REASONABLENESS, LIMIT THE TRIAL STEP TO TRIPLE THE PREVIOUS SUCCESSFUL STEP.
M    IF ABS(STEP) - ABS(3 OLDSTEP) POS, STEP = 3 OLDSTEP
```

```
R          DO NOT ALLOW STEPS TO NEGATIVE L.

M          IF L+STEP NEG, STEP = -.5 L

M          GO TO NEXTSTEP


M          ENDITER   DO TO TOTLSTEP FOR I=0(1)(N-1)

M
S                    SIG  = L  U
                        I    I  I

M
S          TOTLSTEP  X  = X  + SIG
                      I    I      I

M                    F(X) = F(L)

M                    PRINT MSG

M          END OF ITERATION-  F(X),L,SMAG,NCALL / THE N ELEMENTS OF X

M                    PRINT F(X), L, SMAG, NCALL

M
S                    PRINT X   TO X    , SP4
                          0      N-1


R          STOP THE PROGRAM WHEN THE LAST ITERATION WAS SHORTER THAN THE CRITERION (BUT ALLOW AT LEAST N
R          ITERATIONS TO TAKE PLACE).  ALSO IN CASES OF SLOW CONVERGENCE, IT IS NECESSARY TO STOP THE PROGRAM
R          AT SOME MAXIMUM NUMBER OF CALLS OR ITERATIONS.

M          IF L-CRITERION NEG, IF ITERATION-N POS, GO TO NORMEXIT

M          IF NCALL-MAXCALLS POS, GO TO NORMEXIT

M          IF ITERATION-MAXITER POS, GO TO NORMEXIT


R          SAVE THE OLD GRADIENT AND COMPUTE THE NEW GRADIENT.

M          DO TO SAVEG FOR I=0(1)(N-1)

M
S          SAVEG   G(X-SIG)  = G(X)
                           I       I

M          GRADIENT   DO TO GRAD9

M                     DO TO NEWGRAD FOR I=0(1)(N-1)

M                     DO TO XPLUSDL FOR J=0(1)(N-1)

M
S          XPLUSDL   IF J=I, TEMP =X +DL, OTHERWISE TEMP =X
                                  J  J                   J  J
```

200

```
M        CALL FUNCTION, TEMP  TO TEMP
S                           0        N-1
M        RESUME F(X+DL)
M        NCALL = NCALL + 1
M        DO TO XMINDL FOR J=0(1)(N-1)
M  XMINDL IF J=I, TEMP =X  -DL, OTHERWISE TEMP =X
S                     J   J                    J   J
M        CALL FUNCTION, TEMP  TO TEMP
S                           0        N-1
M        RESUME F(X-DL)
M        NCALL = NCALL + 1
M  NEWGRAD G(X)  = ( F(X+DL) - F(X-DL) ) / 2 DL
S             I
M  GRAD9   CONTINUE = CONTINUE

R        THE CHANGE IN GRADIENT IS
M        DO TO YGRAD FOR I=0(1)(N-1)
M  YGRAD  Y  = G(X)  - G(X-SIG)
S          I       I           I

R        THE IMPROVED APPROXIMATION TO THE INVERSE OF THE MATRIX OF SECOND PARTIALS IS
E              N-1
M        SIGY = SUM( SIG  Y )
S               I=0     I  I
M        DO TO NEWHY FOR I=0(1)(N-1)
E              N-1
M  NEWHY  HY   = SUM( H     Y )
S          I     K=0   NI+K  K
E              N-1
M        YHY = SUM( Y  HY )
S         I     I=0   I   I
M        DO TO IMPROVH FOR I=0(1)(N-1)
M        DO TO IMPROVH FOR K=0(1)(N-1)
M  IMPROVH H     = H     + SIG SIG / SIGY - HY HY / YHY
S           NI+K    NI+K      I   K            I  K
```

```
M        GO TO HEADING

R        IN A NORMAL EXIT, THE LAST TRIAL STEP MAY HAVE BEEN A FAILURE.  THEREFORE RESTORE THE BEST DESIGN
R        BY REPEATING THE LAST SUCCESS.

M  NORMEXIT  CALL FUNCTION, X   TO X
S                C    N-1

M        RETURN

M  ABORT1   PRINT MSG, SKIP

M        UNFORTUNATELY THE DIRECTIONAL DERIVATIVE IS UPHILL.  FLETCHER
S        PROMISED THIS COULD NOT HAPPEN.  PUNT.

M        TEMP = SQRT(-1)

M  ABORT2   PRINT MSG, SKIP

E        MINFINDER CAN HANDLE ARRAYS LONGER THAN 10 ONLY IF YOU
M        RE-COMPILE WITH EXTENDED RESERVE STATEMENTS.

M        EXIT

M        START AT ENTER

*  ENDJOB
```

# REFERENCES

Åström, K. J., R. W. Koepcke, and F. Tung (1962), "On the Control of Linear Discrete Dynamic Systems with Quadratic Loss," I. B. M. Research Report RJ-222.

Athans, M., and P. L. Falb (1966), Optimal Control: An Introduction to the Theory and its Applications, McGraw-Hill, New York.

Barnes, J. G. P. (1965), "An Algorithm for Solving Non-Linear Equations Based on the Secant Method," The Computer Journal, Vol. 8, No. 1, pp. 66-72, April.

Bellman, R. E. (1957), Dynamic Programming, Princeton University Press, Princeton, New Jersey.

Bisplinghoff, R. L., H. Ashley, R. L. Halfman (1955), Aeroelasticity, Addison-Wesley, Reading, Mass.

Bryson, A. E., and D. E. Johansen (1965), "Linear Filtering for Time-Varying Systems Using Measurements Containing Colored Noise," IEEE Trans. on Auto. Control, Vol. 10, No. 1, pp. 4-10.

Bryson, A. E. (1966), "Applications of Optimal Control Theory in Aerospace Engineering," 1966 Minta Martin Lecture, Dept. of Aero. and Astro., M. I. T., Cambridge, Mass.

Chang, S. S. L. (1958), "Statistical Design Theory for Digital-Controlled Continuous Systems," AIEE Transactions, Vol. 77, part 2 (Applications and Industry), pp. 191-201, September.

Copps, E. M. (1964), "Powered Flight Phases of CSM; Analytical Description and Mechanization of Steering Equations and the Derivation of CDU Commands," M. I. T. Instrumentation Laboratory, Space Guidance Analysis Memo No. 13-64 (Rev. 1), Cambridge, Mass.

Davidon, W. C. (1959), "Variable Metric Method for Minimization," A. E. C. Research and Development Report, Argonne National Lab. No. 5990 (Rev.).

Deyst, J. J. (1964), "Optimum Continuous Estimation of Non-Stationary Random Variables" (S. M. Thesis), M. I. T. Instrumentation Lab. Report T-369, Cambridge, Mass.

Fisher, J. R. (1966), "Optimal Nonlinear Filtering" (Ph. D. Thesis), Dept. of Eng. Report No. 66-5, University of California, Los Angeles.

Fletcher, R., and M. J. D. Powell (1963), "A Rapidly Convergent Descent Method for Minimization," The Computer Journal, Vol. 6, pp. 163-168, July.

Fletcher, R. (1965), "Function Minimization Without Evaluating Derivatives — A Review," The Computer Journal, Vol. 8, pp. 33-41, April.

Franklin, G. F. (1955), "The Optimum Synthesis of Sampled-Data Systems" (Ph. D. Thesis), Columbia University Electronics Research Lab. Report T-6/B, New York.

Fraser, D. C. (1965), "A Sequence of Computer Programs Useful in the Analysis of Feedback Control Systems," M. I. T. Instrumentation Lab., Report E-1800, Cambridge, Mass.

Gantmacher, F. R. (1959), The Theory of Matrices, Vol. 1 (translated by K. A. Hirsch from the Russian), Chelsea Publishing Co., New York.

Gelfand, I. M., and S. V. Fomin (1963), Calculus of Variations (translated by R. A. Silverman from the Russian), Prentice-Hall, Englewood Cliffs, New Jersey.

Gilbert, E. G. (1963), "Controllability and Observability in Multivariable Control Systems," Jour. Soc. Ind. and Appl. Math., Series A: Control, Vol. 1, No. 2, pp. 128-151.

Gunckel, T. L., and G. F. Franklin (1963), "A General Solution for Linear Sampled-Data Control," ASME Transactions, Jour. of Basic Eng.,85 D, pp. 197-203, June.

Hamming, R. W. (1962), Numerical Methods for Scientists and Engineers, McGraw-Hill, New York.

Hildebrand, F. B. (1956), Introduction to Numerical Analysis, McGraw-Hill, New York.

Ho, Y. C., and R. C. K. Lee (1964), "Identification of Linear Dynamic Systems," Harvard University Cruft Lab. Report TR 446, Cambridge, Mass.

Householder, A. S. (1953), Principles of Numerical Analysis, McGraw-Hill, New York.

James, H. M., N. B. Nichols, and R. S. Phillips (1947), Theory of Servomechanisms, M. I. T. Radiation Lab. Series, Vol. 25, McGraw-Hill, New York.

Jeeves, T. A. (1958), "Secant Modification of Newton's Method," Communications of the Assoc. for Computing Machinery, Vol. 1, No. 8, pp. 9-10, August.

Johansen, D. E. (1964), "Optimal Control of Linear Systems with Complexity Constraints" (Ph. D. Thesis), Harvard University, Cambridge, Mass.

Joseph, P. D., and J. T. Tou (1961), "On Linear Control Theory," AIEE Transactions, Applications and Industry, Vol. 80, pp. 193-196, September.

Joseph, P. D. (1964), "Automatic Rendezvous, Part II: On Board Navigation for Rendezvous Missions," Course notes for "Space Control Systems — Attitude, Rendezvous, and Docking," UCLA Engineering Extension, Los Angeles, Calif.

Kalman, R. E., and R. W. Koepcke (1958), "Optimal Synthesis of Linear Sampling Control Systems Using Generalized Performance Indexes," Trans. ASME, Vol. 80, pp. 1820-1826, November.

Kalman, R. E., and J. E. Bertram (1959), "General Synthesis Procedure for Computer Control of Single-Loop and Multiloop Linear Systems (An Optimal Sampling System)," AIEE Transactions, Vol. 77, Part 2, Applications and Industry, pp. 602-609, January.

Kalman, R. E. (1960), "A New Approach to Linear Filtering and Prediction Problems," Trans. ASME, Series D, Jour. of Basic Eng., Vol. 82, pp. 35-45, March.

Kalman, R. E., and R. S. Bucy (1961), "New Results in Linear Filtering and Prediction Theory," Trans. ASME, Series D, Jour. of Basic Eng., Vol. 83, pp. 95-107, March.

Kalman, R. E. (1963), "Mathematical Description of Dynamic Systems," SIAM Journal on Control, Series A, Vol. 1, No. 2, pp. 152-192.

Lee, R. C. K. (1964), Optimal Estimation, Identification, and Control, The M. I. T. Press, Cambridge, Mass.

Leitmann, G. (1962), Optimization Techniques, with Applications to Aerospace Systems, Academic Press, New York.

Martin, F. H. (1965a), "Closed-Loop Near-Optimum Steering for a Class of Space Missions" (Sc. D. Thesis), M. I. T. Instrumentation Lab., Report T-413, Cambridge, Mass.

Martin, F. H. (1965b), "Programming and Bench Testing of the Digital Filter for the CSM Autopilot," M. I. T. Instrumentation Lab., Space Guidance Analysis Memo 26-65, Cambridge, Mass.

Newton, G. C., L. A. Gould, and J. F. Kaiser (1957), Analytic Design of Linear Feedback Controls, John Wiley, New York.

Pontryagin, L. S., V. G. Boltyanskii, R. V. Gamkrelidze, and E. F. Mishchenko (1962), The Mathematical Theory of Optimal Processes (translated by K. N. Trirogoff from the Russian, edited by L. W. Neustadt), Interscience Publishers, New York.

Potter, J. E. (1964), "A Guidance-Navigation Separation Theorum," M. I. T. Experimental Astronomy Lab., Report RE-11, Cambridge, Mass.

Powell, M. J. D. (1964), "An Efficient Method of Finding the Minimum of a Function of Several Variables Without Calculating Derivatives," The Computer Journal, Vol. 7, pp. 155-162, July.

Ragazzini, J. R., and G. F. Franklin (1958), Sampled-Data Control Systems, McGraw-Hill, New York.

Robinson, A. S. (1957), "The Optimum Synthesis of Computer Limited Sampled Data Systems" (Eng. Sc. D. Thesis), Columbia University, New York.

Rosenbrock, H. H. (1960), "An Automatic Method for Finding the Greatest or Least Value of a Function," The Computer Journal, Vol. 3, pp. 175-184.

Spang, H. A. (1962), "A Review of Minimization Techniques for Nonlinear Functions," SIAM Review 4, pp. 343-365.

Stubbs, G. (1965), "A Block II Digital Lead-Lag Compensation for the Pitch-Yaw Autopilot of the Command and Service Module," M. I. T. Instrumentation Lab. Report R-503, Cambridge, Mass.

Sworder, D. D. (1966), "Control of a Linear Discrete-Time Stochastic System with a Bounded Input," Preprint 1966 Joint Auto. Cont. Conf. (to appear in Jour. of Math. Analysis and Applications).

Traub, J. F. (1964), Iterative Methods for the Solution of Equations, Prentice-Hall, Englewood Cliffs, New Jersey.

Whitman, C. L. (1966), "The Implementation of Digital Filters in Computers of Small Word Length" (S. M. Thesis), M. I. T. Instrumentation Lab. Report T-443, Cambridge, Mass.

Widnall, W. S. (1966a), "On Varying the Gain of Cross-Product Steering Laws to Optimize Short Burn Performance," M. I. T. Instrumentation Lab., Space Guidance Analysis Memo 11-66, Cambridge, Mass.

Widnall, W. S. (1966b), "The Use of Optimal Linear Control Theory to Suggest Digital Autopilot Designs for the Apollo Command and Service Module in Powered Flight," M. I. T. Instrumentation Lab., Space Guidance Analysis Memo 14-66, Cambridge, Mass.

Wiener, N. (1949), Extrapolation, Interpolation, and Smoothing of Stationary Time Series, Technology Press, Cambridge, Mass.

Wolfe, P. (1959), "The Secant Method for Simultaneous Nonlinear Equations," Communications of the Assoc. for Computing Machinery, Vol. 2, No. 12, pp. 12-13, December.

Zadeh, L. A., and C. A. Desoer (1963), Linear System Theory: the State Space Approach, McGraw-Hill, New York.

# INDEX